BIZARRE
BROOKLYN

D1571138

BIZARRE BROOKLYN

Stories of the Tragic, Macabre and Ghostly

ALLISON HUNTINGTON CHASE

THE
History
PRESS

Published by The History Press
Charleston, SC
www.historypress.com

Copyright © 2022 by Allison Huntington Chase
All rights reserved

First published 2022

Manufactured in the United States

ISBN 9781467152396

Library of Congress Control Number: 2022937923

Notice: The information in this book is true and complete to the best of our knowledge. It is offered without guarantee on the part of the author or The History Press. The author and The History Press disclaim all liability in connection with the use of this book.

All rights reserved. No part of this book may be reproduced or transmitted in any form whatsoever without prior written permission from the publisher except in the case of brief quotations embodied in critical articles and reviews.

This book is dedicated to Julia Dakers.

CONTENTS

I'd like to say a special thanks to Matt Zaller.

INTRODUCTION

Brooklyn—the most populous borough in New York City. Birthplace of the Dodgers, Sweet'N Low and Season 21 of *The Real World*. Once named the "coffee capital," Brooklyn is also home to the world's most expensive cup of Joe, which goes for eighteen dollars. Some other things to come out of Brooklyn include Twizzlers, hot dogs, air-conditioning, teddy bears, Mr. Potato Head and the credit card.

Beginning in 1636, this area was first occupied by Native tribes before it was taken over by the Dutch. Originally called Breuckelen, it was made up of small villages and farms. In 1816, Brooklyn officially became its own city. Connecting to Manhattan via the Fulton Ferry, Brooklyn was home to the world's first commuters, thus making Brooklyn the nation's first suburb. A New York City guidebook from 1818 warned visitors "to flee the narrow, dirty and disagreeable place" known as Brooklyn. Yet after the Brooklyn Bridge was constructed, millions of people fled *to* Brooklyn. The Industrial Revolution thrived here. Factories took over the waterfront, creating a vast number of jobs for the growing population.

Brooklyn eventually consolidated with New York City at the turn of the century, which quickly came to be known as the "Great Mistake of 1898." However, if Brooklyn had never joined the city, it would be the fourth-largest city in the United States today. It's larger than Boston; Atlanta; Washington, D.C.; and Minneapolis combined.

With more than four hundred years under its belt, Brooklyn is filled with a history of both sweet and savory moments. So many people have lived and died here, each with their own tale to tell. Both great and gruesome things have taken place here. Some are remembered, and some are forgotten. Yet by revisiting these events, we can bring them back to life. It's through their stories that they continue to live on. After all, they were here before we were.

It's hard to imagine Brooklyn as anything other than a concrete jungle. Who would guess that the first battle of the Revolutionary War was fought here? Literally, almost no one! Lifelong residents of Brooklyn are shocked to discover this historical event, even though it took place right in their backyards! That's why it's so important to keep their stories alive. There are tiny reminders all over the place—it's just that no one knows to look. For instance, right in the middle of Forte Green Park stands the Prison Ship Martyrs Monument. Every day, people come to sit on its steps and take in the views. What they don't know, however, is that it contains the bones of 11,500 people. The information is there on the plaque, but no one even notices it.

To quote the great Ferris Bueller, "If you don't stop and look around once in a while, you could miss it."

PART I.

BROOKLYN BRIDGE

1
CONSTRUCTION AND DESTRUCTION

The Brooklyn Bridge, the "eighth wonder of the world," is the reason Brooklyn is a part of New York City. This iconic and innovative masterpiece connects Brooklyn to Manhattan. Prior to its construction, people relied on ferries to get across the East River. These ferries were atrocious. Due to overcrowding and unsafe conditions, this mode of transportation was both unpredictable and dangerous. For years, talks of a bridge spread throughout New York. After a while, however, the buzz over the rumored bridge became more of pipe dream. Then one day, it was announced that the bridge would be built, and a German immigrant by the name of Roebling would be the one to build it.

Chief engineer John A. Roebling was tasked with designing and constructing the highly anticipated (originally named) East River and Brooklyn Bridge. Not only would this structure revolutionize life in New York City, but it would be the first of its kind. Until then, a suspension bridge of this length did not exist and was thought by some to be impossible.

On June 28, 1869, tragedy struck when Roebling was injured. While walking along the edge of the Fulton Ferry taking last-minute measurements, Roebling caught his right foot in a rope. Unable to free himself, he looked up in horror as he watched the ferry approaching the dock where he was held captive. Frantic and desperate to escape, he tried once again to bolt, but to no avail. The ferry passed by Roebling, crushing his foot along the way. Roebling was taken to the hospital, where he had two of his toes amputated. Shortly following the surgery, his wounds became infected, and he developed tetanus. Twenty-eight days later, he was dead. His thirty-two-year-old son, Washington Roebling, took over as the chief engineer.

The Brooklyn Bridge. *Matt Zaller.*

Washington Roebling was a capable replacement for his father. He studied closely alongside his father (who was said to have beaten him as a child) and fought in Gettysburg during the Civil War. However, it was his wife, Emily Roebling, who was the one to build the bridge after he, too, became a victim of brutal working conditions.

The bridge's construction officially began on January 2, 1870, and took sixteen years and $15 million ($340 million today) to complete. The first obstacle was building the bridge's foundation. In order to do this, workers had to go inside an airtight container called a caisson, which was then lowered to the bottom of the river. To put it bluntly, a caisson was basically a wooden barrel filled with men and explosives. The farther down the caissons went, the more dangerous they became. Due to sudden decompression, men developed "caisson disease" also known as "the bends." This illness caused dizziness, slurred speech, blinding headaches, itchy skin, vomiting, bloody noses, chills, slowed heartbeats, joint pains, paralysis and death. (These are also the symptoms of riding the 6 train at rush hour.) According to E.F. Farrington, the bridge's master mechanic, "The temperature in the caissons was about eighty [degrees], and the workmen, with half-naked bodies, seen in dim, uncertain light brought vividly to life Dante's *Inferno*." Over one hundred men, or "water hogs," as they were nicknamed, suffered

Early construction of the Brooklyn Bridge. *Museum of the City of New York.*

from caisson disease, resulting in deaths and lifelong ailments. While caisson work was well paid, it was not an attractive job due to its dangerous and unpredictable nature. In fact, one-third of caisson workers quit weekly. In the end, more than one hundred people succumbed to caisson disease.

The first person to die from caisson disease was a German man named John Myers. It only took two days of working inside a caisson to kill him.

Grand opening of the Brooklyn Bridge. *Archive.org.*

A week later, an Irish worker named Patrick McKay also passed away. One month later, a man named Daniel Reardon would be the third to die. This dangerous method of work would not just be limited to poor laborers. Washington Roebling would frequently work inside the caissons himself. In 1872, after working inside one for twelve hours straight, he passed out. Roebling became partially paralyzed and bedridden. He would suffer from chronic pain for the rest of his life. Since Roebling was longer able to leave his bedroom, people began to question if he was still capable of continuing with the bridge's construction. A vote was held, and he was allowed to continue on as chief engineer. By using a telescope from his bed, Roebling was able to monitor the construction from his bedroom window. Roebling's wife, Emily, was used to send notes back and forth from Washington to the workers. Emily became quite resourceful and proved to be a crucial element of the bridge's construction. She even taught herself science and math in order to fully understand the mechanisms. While acting as a liaison for her husband, Emily made her way up the ranks and became an official decision maker. She is often credited (and rightfully so) as the real mastermind and unsung hero of the Brooklyn Bridge.

Caisson disease wasn't the only cause of fatalities during the bridge's construction. While moving granite blocks on October 23, 1871, a wooden boom scalped one of the riggers. Another accident occurred when a stonemason was crushed by a mast while his coworker died trying to leap to safety. Other casualties were caused by loose rocks hitting the workers, men falling to their deaths from 275 feet in the air and other workplace accidents. One of the saddest deaths occurred three days before Christmas in 1877, when an Irish widower working as a mason was killed after a temporary wooden arch support gave way, leaving behind five orphans. In total, twenty-seven people died during the construction of the Brooklyn Bridge, though some say the number is as high as forty. (No official record was kept.)

The bridge was officially opened on May 24, 1883, along with fourteen tons of fireworks to help celebrate its completion. The first person to cross the Brooklyn Bridge was Emily Roebling, who carried a rooster on her lap, symbolizing victory. Fifty thousand people followed her. However, Washington Roebling would never step foot on the bridge.

*There's a rumor that says Roebling was hit by the boat on purpose. Since ferries would be losing out on business and money to the new bridge, they wanted to prevent it from being built. (There's no asterisk in the text or a mention of Roebling being hit by a boat. It's a word-of-mouth rumor!)

2

ALIEN ABDUCTIONS

Alien sightings have occurred for thousands of years. They usually take place on farms, along country roads or in deserts. Very rarely, if ever, do we hear about them happening in cities, especially in one as populated as New York. A woman named Linda Napolitano claims it happened to her.

This highly suspicious event took place on November 30, 1989. Around 3:00 a.m., night owl Linda was in the middle of getting ready for bed. She put on her long nightgown, walked inside the bedroom of her twelfth-floor apartment and kneeled down for her nightly prayers. She closed her eyes and began to pray. When she opened them, she saw three gray aliens at the foot of her bed. Frozen in fear, she tried to speak but couldn't. Her body began to levitate. Paralyzed, she began to move toward the closed window. Miraculously, her body floated right through it. The window behind her remained shut. Linda, along with the three gray aliens, were suspended in a blue beam as they made their way to an aircraft that was lingering above the Brooklyn Bridge. Once they were inside, the glowing reddish-orange spaceship flew away in the blink of an eye.

While this story is hard to believe, at least one dozen people have come forward claiming to have seen it happen. (In fact, it has been called the most witnessed alien abduction of all time.) These eyewitnesses, who range in age and gender, claim to have all seen the same thing: a woman in a white nightgown floating through her closed window and into a blue beam of light accompanied by three gray aliens. One of these onlookers was Javier Pérez de Cuéllar, the former secretary general of the United Nations.

View of the Brooklyn Bridge from Manhattan. *Matt Zaller.*

Javier, along with his two bodyguards, all came forward individually to confirm the events.

Linda Napolitano's story went on to inspire the book *Witnessed*, by Budd Hopkins. Her alien encounter has also been featured in *Vanity Fair*, on podcasts and by various news outlets and in artwork.

3
DEADLY SCREAM

Just six days after its grand opening on May 30, 1883, the Brooklyn Bridge was responsible for the deaths of over one dozen people. To be fair, it wasn't exactly the bridge's fault.

At the time of its completion, the Brooklyn Bridge was the longest suspension bridge on Earth. While the bridge was an innovation in architecture, people still doubted its safety. Could it really support the weight of all those people and carriages? Was it safe? Sturdy? Could it collapse? Skepticism and rumors of its instability quickly spread.

On this particular spring day, the city was closed for a federal holiday, giving everyone the day off. A perfect opportunity for the city to visit the most anticipated and famous bridge in the world. Thousands of people gathered at the bridge's entrance and made their way on. For the first time in their lives, they would make the journey from Manhattan to Brooklyn on foot.

The crowd was ecstatic to be there. Decked out in their best attire, they made their way from one borough to the next. Although they were gleeful and eager to be there, they were also extremely worried and paranoid. After all, the bridge was at full capacity. To their surprise and relief, everything seemed to be working fine. Then, suddenly, chaos broke out. As a young woman made her way to the entrance steps, she slipped on the stairs and fell. Another woman who witnessed the slip believed that the bridge was collapsing and let out a scream. A mass panic quickly ensued.

Walking over the Brooklyn Bridge. *Matt Zaller.*

An article from the *New York Star* reported, "At last, with a single shriek that cut through the clamor of thousands of voices, a young girl lost her footing and fell down the lower flight of steps. She lay for a moment and then raised herself on her hands and would have got up. But in another moment, she was buried under the bodies of others who fell over the steps after her. She was dead when they got her out more than half an hour afterward."

The crowd began to rush toward the exits. Grown men pushed children and women out of their way, crawling over them to escape. Others were crushed against the guardrails. Luckily, a worker was able to cut the iron fence, allowing pedestrians to exit the promenade and move onto the streetcar tracks beneath. (The missing piece of the fence can still be seen today.)

A total of twelve people were crushed to death, and dozens were injured. In an article from the *New York Tribune* titled "Brooklyn Bridge Disaster," Robert McNamara said, "A company of the Twelfth New York Regiment worked hard at dragging them out. Twenty-five seemed to be nearly dead. They were laid along the north and south sides of the pathway, and the people from Brooklyn passed on between them. Men and women turned faint at the sight of the swollen and blood-stained faces of the dead. Four men, a lad, six women and a girl of fifteen were quite dead or died in

Aftermath of the Brooklyn Bridge stampede. *Drawing by a staff artist at* Frank Leslie's Illustrated Newspaper, *fair use*.

a few moments. They had been found at the bottom of the heap." The victims were taken to Chambers Street Hospital but not until they had been pickpocketed. The now-empty bridge lay littered with torn clothing, broken watches and canes, jewelry and other personal belongings, some of which was splattered with blood.

In order to prove the bridge's stability, P.T. Barnum led twenty-one elephants over it, directly to his circus on the other side. This went on to inspire the classic children's book *21 Elephants and Still Standing*. Ironically, the bridge was built to hold the weight of more than 2,500 African elephants, having been made six times stronger than necessary.

4
BROOKLYN BRIDGE BOOS

Frank Sinatra once sang about love and marriage: "You can't have one without the other." The same applies to death and ghosts. Where there is death, there are ghosts. The Brooklyn Bridge has plenty of both. Countless people have met their untimely deaths between the bridge's two boroughs—we'll never know how many. Yet their spirits hang around—a common occurrence with tragic, sudden deaths.

One of the most famous ghosts of the bridge is that of a young woman whose sightings have been reported since 1951. Her ghost is described as having long, blond hair and being dressed in a white gown. (Side note: Why are ghosts always wearing long white gowns?) Those who have seen her ghost say it stands by the edge of the bridge crying and looking as if it's about to jump. When they move closer to approach her, it is revealed that she is transparent. Mysterious splashes and screams are also said to be heard when her ghost appears. (The Brooklyn Bridge has always been a popular suicide destination. However, due to its heavy traffic, it's given many people enough time to talk themselves out of it before they arrive at it.)

While Sleepy Hollow, New York, may be home to a headless horseman, the Brooklyn Bridge is home to a headless workman. In 1875 (others claim 1883), a construction worker was decapitated when one of the bridge's cables snapped. Since then, people have claimed to see a headless man walking back and forth on the bridge. Others describe him as a black, shadowy figure. An ominous presence has been reported between the archways in which the accident occurred, as have the sound of his ghostly footsteps.

The bridge through the grass. *Matt Zaller.*

Orbs are often seen on the Brooklyn side of the bridge. Their bright lights shoot through the bridge before vanishing, followed by the sound of loud banging. Perhaps they're the spirits of those unfortunate souls who met their watery ends and decided to stick around.

5

ICE CREAM FIRES

Dating back to the mid-1600s, the land on which Brooklyn Bridge Park stands today was used for boat and ferry transportation. Today, it is one of the most picturesque places in Brooklyn. With crystal clear views of the Brooklyn Bridge and the Manhattan skyline, it's the perfect place to spend the afternoon. However, this grassy and manicured park was the site of many tragedies. Between 1822 and 1952, twenty-six massive fires broke out on this exact spot, claiming the lives of at least eight people. Tragically, another fire occurred here early in 2021, taking the life of an eighty-six-year-old man who was asleep on his boat.

One of the main reasons this area was so prone to fires was its poor design. This congested area was filled with boats and warehouses that were built extremely close together, creating a perfect storm for disaster. According to *Brooklyn Waterfront History*, "Buildings and vessels were crammed with tons of highly combustible goods—tobacco, cotton, coffee, sugar, wool, grain, and dried animal hides." This overcrowding led to an unavoidable recipe for disaster. Just a singular ember could (and would) result in a massive fire.

The first of these tragedies took place on August 21, 1822. The blaze broke out on Furman Street, setting fire to multiple buildings and ships. A firefighter was killed, and $85,000 worth of cotton was burned (the modern equivalent of $1,443,809.13). Forty-two years later, on July 15, 1864, tragedy would strike again. This time, a building on Joralemon Street that was used to store ingredients such as gunpowder combusted into a burst of fire. The blast rose three hundred feet in the air and broke all the windows in Brooklyn

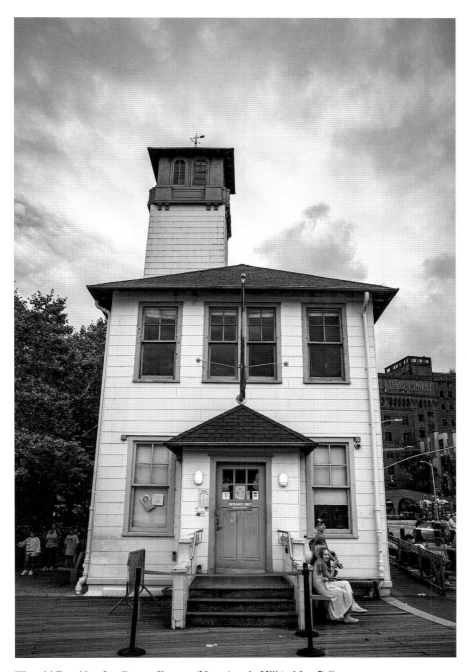

The old Brooklyn Ice Cream Factory (Now Ample Hills). *Matt Zaller.*

Heights. By coincidence, the explosion occurred during their dinner hour, sparing the lives of dock workers who had left the area to eat. This divine intervention resulted in zero deaths from the wreckage.

The next notable fire took place on July 19, 1883. This time, it began on Orange Street and made its way to three cargo ships that had just arrived in New York from Calcutta. The fallout was disastrous. One sailor and dock worker drowned, and a dozen firefighters were injured and killing another. Seventy years later, a two-day fire broke out at the New York Dock Company. The company's warehouse, containing coffee, paper and rubber, was destroyed. In the end, $500,000 worth of goods was lost, and thirty-three firefighters were left injured.

In order to prevent further accidents, the largest fire engine in Brooklyn was stationed near the waterfront in 1888. Then in 1926, the Marine Fire Boat Station was set up in Brooklyn Bridge Park. Today, the station is home to Ample Hills Creamery. (This ice cream company was named after the Walt Whitman poem "Crossing Brooklyn Ferry." In the poem, Whitman described Brooklyn as having "ample hills." What's even more fitting is that Whitman worked directly across the street from Ample Hills Creamery at the *Brooklyn Daily Eagle*.)

PART II

CLINTON HILL

6

LEFFERTS-LAIDLAW HOUSE

Picture it: Brooklyn, 1878.

A house in Clinton Hill is under attack by ghosts. A new invention called a telephone just came out a couple of years ago, but who are we going to call? *Ghostbusters* won't be out for another century!

On December 20, 1878, the *New York Times* published an article about a local haunting in Brooklyn. A house was being plagued by a ghostly game of ding-dong ditch. Ah, yes, ding-dong ditch. Nicknamed "knock, knock, ginger" in England, this annoying yet highly hilarious game has been a childhood tradition since doorbells were first invented. (In this particular case, doorbells had literally just been invented.)

It all began at the home of Edward F. Smith, located at 136 Clinton Avenue. Edward lived there with his family and a couple of tenants he rented rooms out to. One evening, the doorbell rang. When he went to open it, no one was there. After a few minutes, the doorbell rang again. Once again, Edward opened the door to greet no one. Suddenly, the back doors began to be forcefully kicked, banged and rattled. He ran to the back of the house, but the area was unoccupied. The cacophony continued throughout the night. The doorbell and back doors were banged on simultaneously, yet there was no one to be seen. Unfazed, Edward blamed the commotion on the wind and went to bed.

The next day and the day after that—and the day after that—the doorbell rang, someone knocked and the back doors were kicked and banged on. However, there was never anyone in sight. Edward decided to take matters

Lefferts-Laidlaw House. *Matt Zaller.*

into his own hands. He took some flour and ashes and sprinkled it on the walkway and path leading up to the door. However, after another night of torment, there were no footsteps left in the powder.

Edward phoned the police. They came to the house and patrolled the grounds and surrounding area all night. Like clockwork, the ringing and banging commenced out of thin air. The next day, police set up a sting operation and surrounded the house. Finally, the doorbell rang and the police captain himself answered it. Alas, no one was there. Then all of a sudden, a brick was thrown through the dining room window. How was this possible? There were police standing guard in front of it. Skeptical of the situation, a detective came over and ransacked the house. He found nothing. There was no explanation of what could be causing the disturbances. The officers said they were "ready to swear that they have heard and seen the startling demonstrations, and they are morally certain that it is beyond all human probability that any earthly hands pulled the bell, pounded on the doors or threw the brick through the dining room window."

The knocking and ringing continued for the next three weeks. Then one day, it stopped. However, word had gotten around about the supernatural disturbances plaguing the house. Spectators and gawkers began to loiter in front of the house. Psychics and mediums pleaded with Edward to let them in to investigate. He refused, saying, "We consider ourselves perfectly able to take care of any ghost that comes along." Since the spiritualists weren't granted access inside, they began to perform "semi-séances" on the sidewalk. When the police officers began to break up the crowd, the captain was bitten on his finger by a large German man who was determined to stay put.

Rumors spread that the cause of the hauntings was a lawyer who had died by suicide in the home. Edward Smith believed it was the work of Satan. He then claimed to have rid the house of evil through a "long and earnest prayer."

PART III

COBBLE HILL

H.P. LOVECRAFT'S BROOKLYN

Famed sci-fi and horror writer H.P. Lovecraft once lived in Brooklyn and absolutely hated it. He hated it so much, in fact, that he even wrote a story about it called "The Horror at Redhook." Needless to say, you won't find a picture of him sporting an "I ♥ New York" T-shirt.

Lovecraft first moved to Brooklyn in 1924 and only remained there until 1926. However, in this short period, he lost his mind. He described his apartment, located at 169 Clinton Street, as "something unwholesome—something furtive—something vast lying subterrenely [*sic*] in obnoxious slumber—that was the soul of 169 Clinton Street at the edge of Red Hook and in my great northwest corner room."

Today, Cobble Hill is one of the wealthiest neighborhoods in Brooklyn. Its picturesque streets are filled with flowerbeds adorning pristine brownstones, upscale boutiques and overpriced coffeehouses. However, in the 1920s, it was filled with boardinghouses and shanty towns. Overcrowding and filthy conditions made this area a less than desirable place to live. Because of its proximity to the waterfront, this area (then referred to as Red Hook) served as a popular destination for the poor dockworkers, many of whom were immigrants. The neighborhood became known as "Little Syria." This large immigrant population was the leading cause of Lovecraft's loathing of Brooklyn. You see, Lovecraft was a notorious racist and bigot. Simply walking past an immigrant would send him into a meltdown. Some suggest that his hatred for foreigners was so bad that it played a major role in the downfall of his marriage with his wife, Sonia.

H.P. Lovecraft's former home in Cobble Hill. *Matt Zaller.*

"The Horror at Red Hook" was published in 1927 in *Weird Tales* magazine. It describes Brooklyn as the gateway to Hell, led by the occult. In it, Lovecraft wrote, "The population is a hopeless tangle and enigma; Syrian, Spanish, Italian and negro elements impinging upon one another, and fragments of Scandinavian and American belts lying not far distant. It is a babel of sound and filth and sends out strange cries to answer the lapping of oily waves at its grimy piers and the monstrous organ litanies of the harbour whistles." Dramatic much?

While Lovecraft only spent a brief time living in his Brooklyn apartment, it led him to starve himself. "I conceived the idea that the great brownstone house was a malignly sentient thing—a dead vampiric creature that sucked something out of those within it and implanted in them the seeds of some horrible and immaterial psychic growth." It should come as no surprise to anyone that the house is said to be haunted. Another notable tenant who occupied the apartment was Nellie Kurtzman, the daughter of *MAD* magazine's founder, Harvey Kurtzman. Nellie first heard about the empty apartment through her friend who lived in the building. The previous family who lived in the apartment vanished one night, which only made her more intrigued. Wanting to further investigate the ominous and abandoned apartment, Kutzman and her friends decided to hold a séance using a Ouija board. They asked the Ouija board to say something. It spelled out the word *brick*. (One of her friends, a big fan of Lovecraft, had previously taken a brick from the apartment as a memento.) Kurtzman signed the lease. That's when spooky things began to happen.

At first, Nellie started hearing unexplainable noises, especially in the kitchen. Then, bedroom doors would open and close on their own. Items, such as credit cards, would disappear. As soon as she'd order another one, they'd suddenly show up. A hammer would disappear or be moved, and when she hung pictures, they would ricochet off the wall and fall onto the floor. Soon after, Nellie and her roommate began having vivid nightmares. For someone who hated Brooklyn so much, Lovecraft sure insists on sticking around.

TAVERN IN THE WOODS

Can you imagine being at a bar, having the time of your life, when the bartender announces that they've run out of booze? Well, believe it or not, that happened—right here in Brooklyn, no less!

Like most of Brooklyn before the turn of the century, Boerum Hill was all farmland. More specifically, it was the Boerum family's farmland. It's hard to imagine that the location where corner bodegas and Citi Bike racks now stand was once where cows grazed grass. The Boerum family's land was eventually divided and sold, and the "hill" was leveled. One particular parcel of this land was used to build Cobble Hill Fort. This fortress was used in both the Revolutionary War and the War of 1812. Many people died there in battle, and it was quickly rumored to be haunted. For years, it lay in ruins, abandoned among the cornfields past the old potter's field. Fearful of ghosts, locals stayed away from the area, "about which dreadful stories were whispered," according to Henry Read Stiles in *A History of the City of Brooklyn*. By the early 1820s, it was said to be the most haunted place in all of Brooklyn.

Just half a mile from the former fort was a charming home that belonged to the actress Charlotte Melmoth. After retiring from the stage, she spent her remaining years working as a children's tutor. When she passed away in 1826, the property was transformed from a home into a frat house (figuratively speaking). Young men, old men, farmers, dock workers, women of the night and everyone in between gathered at this wooden tavern. It was basically the 1800s' version of Studio 54. They drank until they were belligerent, shucked oysters and smoked their pipes.

One night, around 11:00 p.m., the bar ran out of brandy. Not wanting the night's festivities to end, the men became—emotional. They were outraged and desperate. But wait! There were more bottles of brandy close by on the ferries. They could be back to drinking in no time! The only problem was that they'd have to pass by the haunted fort on the way.

Joseph Moser, an eyewitness, described what took place in the book *A History of the City of Brooklyn*, saying:

> *One night, while a party of young roysterers were assembled at the tavern, having what is best described as a high old time, it was suddenly discovered that the supply of brandy had given out. As the new supply of the desired fluid could only be procured by going down to Brooklyn ferry for it, it immediately became an important question who would go for it; inasmuch as nearly all present shared an apprehension (which, however, they are not willing to own) about passing the haunted house alone at that time of night, it being past eleven o'clock. At length, a young man named Boerum volunteered his services, boasting that he was not afraid of a ghost and (with forced hardihood) declaring even his desire to meet it. Mounting his horse, therefore, he started for the ferry after the brandy. An hour elapsed and still another, but he returned not. His boon companions, becoming uneasy in consequences of his prolonged absence, finally resolved to go, all together, and seek him. Mounting, not in hot haste, however, they returned their horses' heads towards the village and on approaching the haunted ground, they found young Boerum's horse standing against the fence not far from the house, and when they reached the spot itself, their companion was discovered lying senseless in the road, with his features horribly distorted. He was taken back to the tavern, where he lingered for two or three days in a speechless condition and then died.*

To quote a sacred New Yorker, Carrie Bradshaw, "I couldn't help but wonder," was this the work of a ghost or the consequence of riding a horse drunk in the middle of the night?

TUNNEL TO NOWHERE

Atlantic Avenue is one of the most famous avenues in Brooklyn. It even has its own festival every year. Thousands of runners race on top of it annually for the New York Marathon, alongside the endless small businesses, restaurants, coffee shops and bars. However, it's what lies underneath the avenue that's really worth mentioning.

Unknown to many, beneath its pavement lies the oldest subway in the world. Commissioned by Cornelius Vanderbilt in 1884, the Atlantic Avenue Tunnel was designed for a smoother, faster and less–accident prone ride. Yet while the train was an innovation, it was only in operation for sixteen years.

The Atlantic Avenue Tunnel was built in just seven months by Irish immigrants using primitive hand tools. Yet in this short time, a murder and cover-up took place. In 1844, the *Brooklyn Daily Eagle* published an article claiming that a British man was shot after ordering the Irish-Catholic laborers to work on Sundays, which would prevent them from going to church. Outraged, one of the men shot him. With the help of his coworkers, the Irish man buried the British man's body behind a plastered wall. Another thing concealed within the tunnel is an 1830s locomotive in perfect condition. According to *Bklyner*, the tunnel's other hidden items include "missing pages of John Wilkes Booth's diary, pirates, prohibition era bootleggers, mustard gas–wielding World War II spies, mobsters and giant water rats." H.P. Lovecraft even wrote about Persian vampires roaming its halls.

The tunnel was eventually closed in 1861, after the New York State Legislature banned railroad locomotives in Brooklyn. The reason for this

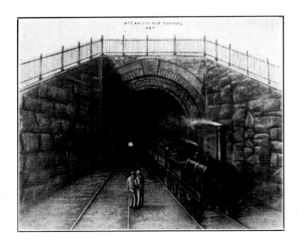

The Atlantic Avenue Tunnel.
Photographer unknown, 1844.

ban? One of the major shareholders in the competing Long Island Railroad, John A. King, just happened to be the governor of New York at the time.

In 1980, a man named Bob Diamond discovered the abandoned and virtually forgotten tunnel. For the next several months, he obsessed over uncovering it. After much research and physical labor, Diamond was able to make his way inside. For many years, he would lead tours throughout the tunnel until city officials deemed it to be unsafe. Another way of getting into the tunnel is through the restaurants lining Atlantic Avenue. Many of the basements have secret entrances leading to the tunnel. One establishment even turned its hidden passage into a speakeasy.

PART IV

CONEY ISLAND

10

FREAKSHOWS AND FRIGHTS

The only thing about America that interests me is Coney Island.
—Sigmund Freud, 1909

Coney Island, originally referred to as Rabbit Island by the Dutch, is really a peninsula that was first discovered by Henry Hudson in 1609. By the 1820s, it became known as Coney Island, an upscale seaside resort. When the beaches were opened to the public, its popularity soared. New train lines were installed, allowing easy access for the general public. This once exclusive community was now available to everyone, resulting in up to one million people coming to the beach each day.

When the boardwalk opened in 1923, it was labeled as "Coney Island's Fifth Avenue." However, Coney Island wasn't always a glitz-and-glamour destination. (In fact, that might be the first time the words *Coney Island* and *glamour* have ever been used in the same sentence.) The area quickly became filled with seedy pockets known as "Coney Island's Bowery." One of the main landmarks on this side of the "island" (nicknamed "Sodom by the Sea") was the Elephantine Colossus, a hotel known for its prostitution. If you were able to "see the elephant," it meant you were in the bad part of town.

Many inventions came out of Coney Island, such as the hot dog (1867)* and the roller coaster (1884). Frozen custard was also invented here in 1919 as a solution to fast-melting ice cream. It was an instant hit. Within the first week alone, eighteen thousand frozen custards were sold. As the amusement parks expanded, new rides and attractions followed. These

Coney Island in 1929.
Photographer: Edward J. Kelty, fair use.

rides were unstable and, therefore, unsafe. (If you've ever been on a wooden roller coaster, you know they're also uncomfortable.) One of these rides was Roosevelt's Rough Riders. In 1910, tragedy struck when sixteen people were ejected from the ride, killing three of them. The entertainment didn't stop there. Even celebrities, such as Harry Houdini and Buffalo Bill, came to perform their shows on Coney Island.

Coney Island is, even today, is synonymous with freak shows. Beginning in 1880, these sideshows mostly consisted of human oddities. For a nickel, you could see the bearded lady, the lion-faced man or the four-legged woman. If you were missing a limb or had an extra, Coney Island could provide you with a lucrative career and a built-in community. Basically, anyone who could be exploited would be exploited. Decades later, these sideshows were considered distasteful and degrading, leading to a decline in their popularity. Unfortunately, the performers were the ones who suffered most, and they found themselves out of work.

In 1904, the sideshow was introduced, starting a grim trend. Aside from innocuous acts, such as sword swallowing or lion taming, most of these shows featured minorities who were put on display like zoo animals. The first of these shows was *Lilliputia*, which was a half-scale city designed for little people. Nicknamed the "Midget City," the exhibit consisted of a functioning fire department, a private beach with lifeguards and even its own parliament. Perhaps the most inhumane sideshows included "human zoos." These exhibits were made up of "primitive natives" hailing from the Philippines to the Congo.

The most controversial sideshow was made up of premature babies. Incubators, while effective, were not used in hospitals around the turn of the century. A man named Dr. Martin Couney, recognizing the machine's potential, purchased many of them. Mothers, desperate to keep their babies alive, flocked to Coney Island for a chance of saving their children inside one of these machines. The tradeoff for using an incubator was that the baby would be put on display to the public. For the price of a ticket, one could view these small babies and gawk at their tiny appearances. While this was borderline inhumane, it provided lifesaving technology for these newborns. In total, 8,000 babies were brought to Coney Island. The sideshow saved the lives of 6,500 of them.

Of course, given Coney Island's colorful past, ghosts have taken up residence here. A popular wedding venue and event space called Oriental Manor was known for its hauntings. Rumor has it that it was haunted by three different ghosts. Its doors opened and closed on their own, and the sound of phantom footsteps were a common occurrence. While it was later converted into a discount department store, the ghosts remain loyal residents.

*Hot dog sellers hired doctors to eat hot dogs in front of their stand to convince people they were healthy.

PART V

DOWNTOWN BROOKLYN

11

BROOKLYN THEATER FIRE

On the night of December 5, 1876, the Brooklyn Theater was putting on a performance of *The Two Orphans*, starring Harry S. Murdock and Kate Claxton. The theater, which had been built only five years earlier, was a marvel in architecture. Its red velvet seats added to the ornate interior. With the theater located at the intersection of Johnson and Washington Streets, Brooklyn's crème de la crème congregated here to see the latest plays. (Today, Johnson and Washington Streets no longer exist. The land is now home to a park called Cadman Plaza.)

On this particular evening, the theater was at full capacity, with all nine hundred of its seats filled. The show started out as planned, capturing the attention of the audience, who delighted in the theatrics. Then, around 11:00 p.m., things went horribly wrong. A gaslamp fell, setting fire to some props backstage. The stagehands tried to put it out but failed. Not only was there no hose, but there wasn't even a bucket to put water in. Smoke began to come out from the side of the stage. At first, the audience assumed it was part of the play, and the actors remained in character. However, as the fire began to spread, someone noticed flames and yelled, "Fire!" When the actors started to leave the stage themselves, panic ensued. Within ten minutes, the entire theater was on fire.

Fire exits and safety protocols were not enforced at the time and were often overlooked. This meant that there were only a few doors through which to escape. However, only one of them was open. While some people were able to exit through the main door, many people were not as lucky.

1. Out of the Depths. 2. Death at the Window. 3. A Leap From the Gallery. 4. Registering the Missing. 5. Nursing the Injured.
NEW YORK.—THE BURNING OF THE BROOKLYN THEATRE, DECEMBER 5TH—SCENES AND INCIDENTS OF THE TERRIBLE DISASTER.

Brooklyn theater fire. *From* Frank Leslie's Illustrated Newspaper.

A stampede formed, crushing (mostly) women and children. The balcony section, consisting mostly of working-class ticket holders, became jampacked with people attempting to escape. A survivor told the *New York World* that he witnessed "women screaming, pushed aside by rough-looking men and boys.…I saw a large, rough man who appeared to be blind from excitement jump over the heads nearest to him and come down on the face of a fallen woman. The sight sickened me."

The head usher ran to an alley door and tried to open it. However, these doors were often kept locked in order to keep theater crashers out. He was eventually able to pry it open, but the plan backfired when a burst of air coming through the door made the fire spread even faster. The fire grew so big that firefighters had to wait until it calmed down around 3:00 a.m. to get inside. By that time, nearly the entire building had been destroyed. When the firefighters entered, they found around 300 bodies so badly burned that they had all melted together. It would take weeks to collect all the bodies, which were believed to number somewhere between 283 and 350. The victims' bodies were set up in a viewing gallery by the coroner so that family members and friends could identify them. Unfortunately, there were 103 bodies that were left unidentified. A public funeral was held at Green-Wood Cemetery, where the anonymous bodies were buried. A large statue dedicated to the victims of the Brooklyn Theater Fire stands there today.

The play's leading actress, Kate Claxton, survived and was found early the next morning wandering around Manhattan in a state of shock. Claxton's

Brooklyn Theater Fire Monument at Green-Wood Cemetery. *Matt Zaller.*

fame grew tremendously due to the fire's notoriety, but she would suffer from PTSD for the rest of her life. As for the leading man, Harry S. Murdock? Well, he decided that before escaping, he would first comb his hair and change his clothing. Unfortunately, he took too long, and the floor collapsed beneath him, causing him to fall to his death.

The owners decided to rebuild a new theater on the same spot, much to the opposition of the public. Renamed Haverly's Theatre, this elaborate building did not draw the same crowds that the previous structure drew. The reason? People believed it was haunted by the victims of the Brooklyn Theater fire. From the outside, locals claimed to see glowing lights coming through the windows. On the inside, a custodian witnessed ghost actors on stage, reciting lines from *The Two Orphans*, the play that was being performed the night of the fire. He quit soon after, as did his fellow coworkers.

The *Pittsburgh Dispatch* wrote an article on April 27, 1890, describing the lack of attendees at the new theater due to its haunted reputation: "Superstitious dread arose during the past winter. It was declared, nobody knows by whom at first, but by a great many later on, that every gallery seat was nightly occupied by the ghost of the person whose life had been lost there in the fire."

A few days later, the eleven-year-old theater was knocked down and eventually turned into Cadman Plaza. However, the theater's story lives on. A century later, in 1981, folk singer June Lazare wrote a song called "The Brooklyn Theater Fire," keeping its memory alive.

The Brooklyn Theater fire is ranked as the third-worst theater fire in history. The *National Republican* newspaper even labeled it as "Brooklyn's Holocaust."

PART VI

FLATBUSH

12

HIGH SCHOOL HAUNTS

Erasmus Hall High School is the oldest high school in New York State, which is why it is also called the "mother of high schools." Built by the Dutch in 1786 with the help of Alexander Hamilton and Aaron Burr, Erasmus Hall High School has been a resident of Brooklyn for 235 years. The building itself is gigantic and was designed to mimic the campuses of Oxford and Cambridge Universities. Needless to say, the school building, originally built in a former village, stands out like a sore thumb in the bustling urban Brooklyn streets. As the years went by, more buildings were erected in an elaborate Gothic style, featuring original Tiffany stained-glass windows.

The school was officially opened in 1787 and had only twenty-six students. (It wasn't until 1801 that it would start accepting female students.) Famous alumni include Barbra Streisand, Neil Diamond, Bobby Fischer, Mae West and Clive Davis. Moe Howard attended the school as well until he left to pursue his career in *The Three Stooges*. And while these famous faces have walked the halls, Erasmus Hall High's reputation became more and more dangerous as the years went by. Multiple students were murdered inside the school due to the violence in the school for over one hundred years. In January 1922, a fourteen-year-old boy named Harold Cisney died due to a fight that occurred inside the school. He had been punched and then fell, hitting his head on the cement floor. He died a few days later. Then in December 2011, a fifteen-year-old boy named Alfredo Allen died after being stabbed multiple times with scissors during a lunchtime basketball dispute.

Erasmus Hall Courtyard. *Matt Zaller.*

It should come as no surprise that Erasmus Hall High School is notoriously haunted. Another famous former student is actor Michael Rapaport. During a guest appearance on *Celebrity Ghost Stories*, Michael described a terrifying experience he had in the eleventh grade. He and his friend Gerald were in detention one afternoon when they were ordered by the principal to go clean the basement. They were handed the keys, unlocked the padlock and went inside. When the door closed behind them, they thought nothing of it, since they had the lock and keys in their hand.

The room was filled with wooden desks piled on top of one another. On the floor were cat carcasses. The room was noticeably colder than the hallway, even though there were no windows. Freezing cold. Gerald, who is of Hatian descent, began to panic. He could sense there were spirits in the room and desperately wanted to leave. Suddenly, the lights began to flicker. Then all the desks began to crash onto the floor, creating massive amounts of dust. Through the commotion and debris, Michael saw the figure of a little boy smirking behind it. The boy moved quickly around the room. Michael and Gerald began to freak out and ran to the door. They pulled at the knob, but the door wouldn't open. It couldn't have been locked since they still had the padlock and keys with them, which accelerated their fear. Finally, the door opened, and Gerald ran up the stairs.

Decades after the incident, which both the men claimed they were "traumatized" by, Michael and Gerald revisited the location. This time, they were accompanied by psychic-medium Kim Russo. As they retraced their steps, she gave them a reading. During the investigation, they made contact with both Harold and Alfredo. When they made their way back into the room with the desks had fallen, Russo declared that the boy Michael and Gerald had seen in detention had died in that room after freezing to death.

13

MELROSE PARK

Are you superstitious? Do you believe in ghosts? Whether you do or not,
there are hundreds, yes, thousands, of persons living in the Flatbush district
of Brooklyn who do and who will tell you there is no doubt at all about
the existence of the ghost of Melrose Hall.
—Brooklyn Daily Eagle, *1895*

Melrose Hall, a house so full of murder and mystery it should be called Melrose Place. This grand home was, as the newspaper once described it, "gloomy, deserted and surrounded by the superstitious dread with which tradition has clothed it." Built in 1749 for Colonel William Axtell, it was one of the finest homes in the country. Axtell, whose family could be traced back to Cromwell's army, was an avid Loyalist and member of the King's Council. During the Revolutionary War, the home served as a meeting place for fellow Tories. It also served as a prison for American soldiers, whom Axtell notoriously tortured. According to an article in the *Brooklyn Daily Eagle* from 1884, "Beneath the mansion are the dungeons, dark vaults into which the light of day never penetrates, where prisoners were confined during the Revolution." For years, rumors said that ghostly howls and cries of desperation could be heard from outside of the home. Axtell also enslaved many people, who lived and worked in the home. Years later, when the home was surveyed, hidden prison cells filled with several skeletons and chains were discovered.

Melrose Park in 1912. *Brooklyn Historical Society.*

The legend states that Axtell, a married man with two children, fell madly in love with a servant named Isabella. (Some say she was a Native princess who saved him from capture.) She is described as "a tall, dark woman of wondrous beauty and kindly manner." Axtell kept Isabella hidden inside a secret chamber above the ballroom, away from his wife and the rest of the household. The only other person who knew of Isabella's existence was an enslaved woman named Miranda. Miranda was ordered to help keep Isabella hidden and was in charge of looking after her. She fed and clothed her and took care of her every need. Then at nighttime, Miranda would unlock Isabella's chamber and bring her to the library. There, Isabella and Axtell would sit by the fireplace and spend time together.

One night, Axtell informed Isabella that he had been summoned in response to an "Indian attack" on the frontier. He told her he would be gone for at least a year. Isabella worried about what was to become of her, but Axtell assured her that Miranda would keep her safe while she awaited his return. He left the next day.

Every day, as promised, Miranda would go up the hidden staircase to Isabella's room with supplies. The seasons went by, and Axtell was due back soon. Then suddenly, Miranda fell ill. As she lay dying in her bed, Miranda desperately tried to warn the others of Isabella. Who was Isabella? What hidden chamber? Miranda must be hallucinating! The other enslaved people dismissed her pleas and blamed them on her fever and old age. Miranda died the next evening. Isabella, unaware of Miranda's passing, waited for her to come with some food and water. Hours turned into days with no Miranda in sight. Isabella screamed and banged on the walls, begging for help. Her stomach growled, and her throat went dry as she grew weaker and weaker, until she eventually died from starvation alone inside the room.

News of Axtell's arrival reached Melrose Hall, and an elaborate celebration was planned. When he arrived at home, he was eagerly greeted by his loved ones. He hugged and kissed everyone and indulged in food and festivities. Suddenly, Isabella popped into his head. He missed her and was excited to reunite. Axtell scanned the room, looking for Miranda. When he could not find her, he asked one of the servants where she was. "She died six weeks ago," they informed him. Axtell's face went pale. If Miranda was dead, who was taking care of Isabella? He ran to the hidden staircase and unlocked the secret chamber. Isabella's body fell out onto the ground in front on his feet. He dropped down to his knees, crying into her corpse.

A few nights later, as he sat with his family at the dinner table, all the candles were blown out. According to a newspaper article from October 13, 1895:

> *Suddenly, the secret passage opened, and the spectral form of Isabella entered. The face was ashen pale, each vein strongly defined on the emaciated features, her long black hair hung drooping over her shoulders to the floor, and she seemed clad in airy gossamer. The apparition bore the look of unutterable sorrow, and the hands were clenched in an attitude of woe. Noiselessly then glided through the hall—her sightless eyeballs bent on the petrified form of the colonel, while the lips moved in a ghastly smile as the bony hand pointed to the trembling wife. Nearing the entrance to the secret stairs, she turned and, with her finger, wrote the word* betrayer, *then vanished.*

The room went dark once again. Then a scream was heard. When the family lit the candles once more, they saw Axtell covered in blood. He had been stabbed in the heart with his own sword.

Since then, it was said that Isabella's ghost was seen whenever there is a party in the ballroom, gliding through the room before vanishing into thin air. The home went through various owners before being demolished in 1903, and the land was turned into Prospect Lefferts Gardens.

PART VII

GOWANUS

14

BODIES OF WATER

If you mention the Gowanus Canal, eight times out of ten, it will be followed by a chuckle. That's because this one-and-a-half-mile-long canal is infamous—infamously disgusting, that is. In fact, it even has its own gift shop, with numerous posters featuring a fictitious monster "from" the Gowanus Canal. (Think "Toxic Avenger.")

Gowanus dates to the settlement of the Dutch in the 1600s and was only a small creek. While the waterway was tiny, the oysters that grew there were gigantic, with some measuring up to a foot in length. For a while, Gowanus's famous oysters supplied most of Europe and served as the area's main export. New York Harbor served as the perfect environment for these shellfish. With 220,000 acres of oyster beds, the harbor had almost half of Earth's population of oysters. By the turn of the century, more than one billion oysters were collected each year. (There's a modern program called the Billion Oyster Project that plans on getting one billion oysters back in New York Harbor by 2035.) In 1869, the Gowanus Canal was created and quickly became one of the busiest waterways in America. This commercial and industrial hub was incredibly successful, shipping six million tons of goods each year until it stalled out almost one hundred years later in the 1960s.

Now, let's talk about the water—or should I say "water." Nicknamed "Lavender Lake," the canal is also known for its colorful, chemical waste hues. Due to algae feeding on human excrement, the canal can also occasionally turn green. Aside from its iridescence, the water has tested

Above: A view of the Gowanus Canal from the Carroll Street Bridge under construction. *Matt Zaller.*

Left: The early Gowanus Canal. *Courtesy of the Museum of the City of New York.*

positive for mercury, cholera, pesticides, typhus, typhoid and gonorrhea—oh, and the occasional human body. There is also an unidentified substance in the water, which was officially named "black mayonnaise." Another mystery material found in the canal is something called "white goo," made up of protozoans, bacteria and other contaminants. In 2010, the canal was designated an EPA Superfund Site. The main reason for this was the fact that the Gowanus Canal was basically Brooklyn's toilet. In 1910, the water was described as being almost solid with sewage.

The occasional aquatic life takes up residence in the canal. In 1928, an eighteen-foot-long sperm whale entered the canal, and its carcass was later put on display at the Museum of Natural History after it was killed. In 1952, a shark made its way into the canal before being shot by police. Then in

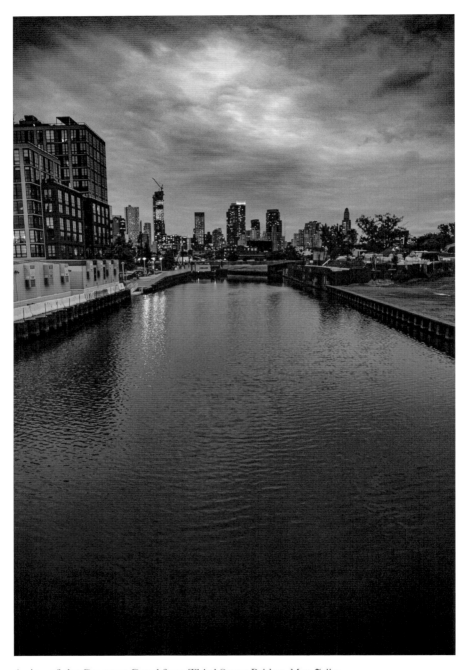

A view of the Gowanus Canal from Third Street Bridge. *Matt Zaller.*

2007, a baby minke whale was spotted in the canal. Unfortunately, it was only in the water only twenty-four hours before dying and was nicknamed "Sludgie the Whale," after Carvel "Fudgie the Whale" ice cream cake.

The Gowanus Canal was also the inspiration for another ice cream, this time from Ample Hills Creamery. Named "It Came from Gowanus," the ice cream "tells the story of an imagined movie monster emerging from the polluted canal. Full of deep, dark mystery and endless surprises, this flavor is a salty dark chocolate ice cream mixed with orange-scented brownies, hazelnut crack'd cookies and white chocolate pearls (an homage to the oysters tasked with cleaning up the waterway)."

I think it's safe to say that it's better to eat the canal's ice cream than its oysters.

15

BATTLE OF BROOKLYN

Whenever I tell people that the first battle of the Revolutionary War occurred in Brooklyn, they don't believe me. It's hard to imagine this concrete jungle as a battlefield. Not only was it the first battle of the Revolutionary War, but it was also the largest and bloodiest. Known as the Battle of Brooklyn, it is also referred to as the Battle of New York or the Battle of Long Island.*

Following America's Declaration of Independence from King George (now celebrated with the Fourth of July), the first battle was fought on August 27, 1776. The land the fighting took place on now comprises Prospect Park, Gravesend Bay, Battle Hill (also known as Green-Wood Cemetery), Fort Greene Park, Fulton Ferry and Gowanus. The headquarters for George Washington's Continental army was located in the Old Stone House, a 1699 Dutch farmhouse. While the original building did not survive, a replica was built in the 1930s as part of the New Deal and is located in Washington Park on the border of Gowanus and Park Slope.

From the very beginning, this battle was not a fair fight. Britain had the super army of the world, and America…did not. In fact, out of the initial 1,200 American soldiers who signed up, only 4 had military training. The army began to dwindle in size when recruits ran off and deserted their duties out to fear. An additional 400 soldiers were brought in from Maryland to help fight in the battle. Known as the "Maryland 400," most of these soldiers were teenagers, sons of rich merchants, schoolboys, laborers and even freed enslaved people. These 400 men went up against 2,000 British

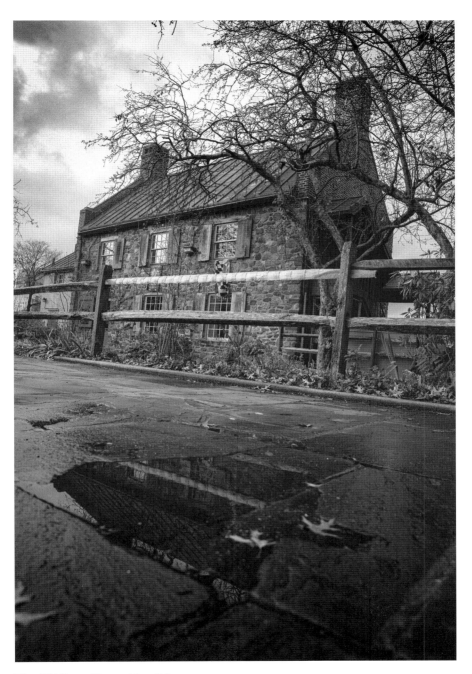

The Old Stone House. *Matt Zaller.*

Battle at the Old Stone House. *Courtesy of the Old Stone House Museum.*

A close-up of the Maryland Four Hundred Monument in Prospect Park. *Matt Zaller.*

IN HONOR OF
MARYLAND'S FOVR HVNDRED
WHO ON THIS BATTLE-FIELD
AVGVST 27ᵀᴴ 1776
SAVED THE AMERICAN ARMY

The Maryland Four Hundred
Monument in Prospect Park. *Matt Zaller.*

soldiers. Needless to say, America lost. However, the battle was not fought in vain. It is because of their sacrifice that the Revolutionary War wasn't over on day one. The 400 Maryland soldiers continued to fight in order to distract the British, allowing George Washington to escape to Manhattan via canoe on the East River, and continue the war. "Good God! What brave fellows I must lose this day!" Washington cried as he watched the young men fall to their deaths.

Out of the 400 Maryland soldiers, 256 were killed and the rest were captured or beaten. The soldiers' dead bodies were thrown into a pit located next to the Old Stone House by the British and forgotten about for centuries. By the time the location of their mass grave was discovered, it was too late. A Staples office supply store was built on top of it.

In the end, one thousand American lives were lost, while only four hundred British soldiers died. On September 15, 1776, Britain officially captured New York, occupying it for the next seven years until they sailed away after defeat in 1783. And it is because of these brave men that Starbucks is a coffee shop and not a tea shop.

*Long Island is technically a part of Brooklyn.

PART VIII

GREEN-WOOD CEMETERY

16

BROOKLYN'S FINEST

In 1860, New York State's number one tourist attraction was Niagara Falls. The second-most popular attraction was Green-Wood Cemetery, bringing in more than half a million visitors a year. There was no Statue of Liberty, Empire State Building or Central Park to visit. In fact, there were not even parks. This then-rural graveyard was the only manicured land in the city one could enjoy. Everyone from families picnicking to artists displaying their paintings frequented the grassy graveyard.

Built in 1838 on the highest natural peak in Brooklyn, Green-Wood Cemetery provides breathtaking views of the Manhattan skyline. The grounds comprise more than 478 acres and are home to over 570,000 graves (or as Green-Wood calls them, "permanent residents").

As the population of New York City grew, burial space shrank. This overcrowding of corpses in churchyards and on city land led to disease outbreaks among the living. A larger burial spot would have to be built in order to solve the problems of limited space and unsanitary conditions. Green-Wood Cemetery would be the answer. However, when its gates first opened (which would eventually be melted for ammunition during World War II), it was not as prestigious as it is today. Due to the fact that Brooklyn was still a separate city from New York, the location was thought of as a second-tier area. That all changed when an agreement was made to relocate the body of Erie Canal creator DeWitt Clinton from Albany to Green-Wood. This publicity stunt encouraged many other public figures to be buried here, turning it into a celebrity hot spot of sorts. "It is the ambition of the New

The entrance to Green-Wood Cemetery. *Matt Zaller.*

Yorker to live upon Fifth Avenue, to take his airings in the park and to sleep with his fathers in Green-wood," read an 1866 *New York Times* article.

Everyone from actors, musicians and inventors to politicians and war generals—even a dog—are buried here. Some familiar names include Leonard Bernstein (composer), Jean-Michel Basquiat (artist), Boss Tweed (corrupt politician), Charles Lewis Tiffany (Tiffany & Co.), William Merritt Chase (artist), Charles Ebbets (Dodgers owner), William "Bill the Butcher" Poole (Bowery Boy), Frederick August Otto Schwarz (FAO Schwarz), Henry Steinway (pianist), Frank Morgan (*The Wizard of Oz*), Elias Howe (the inventor of the sewing machine) and Charles Feltman (the inventor of the hot dog).

One of the more controversial graves within these hallowed grounds belongs to tobacconist John Anderson. And by grave, I mean massive mausoleum. Toward the end of his life, Anderson claimed to be haunted by his former employee, Mary Rogers. She had been hired to work for him in 1838 in the hopes of luring customers in with her good looks and would soon become known as the "beautiful cigar girl." Anderson became infatuated with Mary to the point of obsession. The story took a strange turn when, later that year, Mary went missing after leaving behind a suicide note. She returned a short while later, claiming to have been away visiting a friend in Brooklyn. While there was no official answer about exactly what happened,

A view of the Green-Wood Cemetery. *Matt Zaller.*

the event was believed to have been a publicity stunt for the cigar store. However, three years later, in 1841, Mary disappeared once again. This time, her body was found floating in the Hudson River. Understandably, all eyes immediately went to Anderson. Nonetheless, no arrests were made, and the murder of Mary Rogers was never solved. In 1881, Anderson died of pneumonia while in Paris. Before dying, he claimed to be haunted by Mary's ghost. Her tale would not be forgotten, inspiring Edgar Allan Poe's "The Mystery of Marie Rogêt."

While Green-Wood is still an active cemetery, available burial plots are difficult to come by. Considering how many important people are laid to rest there, the cemetery's standards are high. For instance, it was ruled that no one who has died in jail or been executed for a crime can be buried there. However, anyone is able to take their secrets to the grave inside its gates. *Here Lie the Secrets of the Visitors of Green-Wood Cemetery* is an installation by artist Sophie Calle. Visitors are able to write down their deepest, darkest secrets and slip them inside the obelisk, after which they are periodically taken out and burned.

PART IX

NAVY YARD

17

NAVY HOSPITAL

The Brooklyn Navy Yard Hospital is, hands down, the most historic and (arguably) important hospital in Kings County and has served the residents (and enemies) of Brooklyn since its doors first opened more than two hundred years ago. In 1904, it was named one of the best hospitals in the country. The Navy Yard Hospital revolutionized surgery and modern medicine. In the 1850s, a young doctor named E.R. Squibb invented anesthesia inside the hospital's laboratory, forever changing the course of medical history.

Today, when we think of hospitals, we picture sterile floors and the smell of bleach. The original Navy Yard Hospital was the complete opposite. According to an 1811 report, the hospital was located on a "pond," which resulted in the hospital flooding whenever the high tide came in. The fact that there were no sanitation precautions made the hospital a cesspool of germs and bacteria. A new building was later constructed in 1831, which was intended to treat sailors. There were 125 beds with a capacity of 150 patients. By the beginning of the Civil War, the hospital was able to accommodate 450 patients. Aside from the main building, there were also surgeon and nursing residences, a laboratory and a cemetery.

The Navy Yard Hospital played a crucial role during wartime, starting from the Revolutionary War and continuing to World War II. During the Civil War, the Naval Hospital supplied one-third of the medicine for Union soldiers and treated one-fourth of the Union army's injured soldiers. The

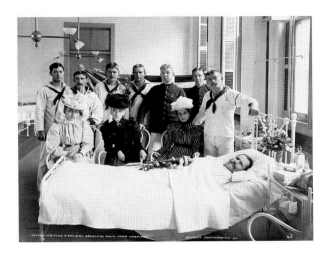

Inside the Brooklyn Navy Yard Hospital, 1890s. *The Library of Congress.*

basement, however, was used as a prison for Confederate soldiers. Needless to say, many people died inside its walls. During World War II, the Navy Yard Hospital provided one-half the medical supplies used in combat.

In the 1840s, an American ship was attacked while in the Pacific. Ten men were killed and then eaten. This cannibalistic attack was led by Fijian Chief Vendovi, who was soon after captured and shipped to New York. While waiting for the ship to drop anchor, a man named Charles Pickering wrote to Dr. Samuel George Morton, an avid skull collector, alerting him of Vendovi's arrival. "Our Feejee Cheif [*sic*] is on his last legs and will probably give up the ghost tomorrow." A few days after arriving in America, Chief Vendovi died from tuberculosis in June 1842. (News reports would blame his death on "consumption in consequence probably of having no human flesh to eat.") Vendovi's head was then removed and embalmed. A death mask was made of his face and displayed in the hospital's main entrance for many years. His skull, an infamous prized possession, went on to Washington, D.C. (it's believed to be kept at the Smithsonian), and his body was buried in an unmarked grave somewhere in Brooklyn.

The hospital was closed in 1948 and neglected for decades. The hospital's once pristine residences began to crumble, and graffiti covered the exposed brick. It became a ghost of Brooklyn's past. Then in 2004, the hospital was purchased by Steiner Studio to build sets for *Saturday Night Live*. Designers and carpenters who work in the building late at night sometimes feel an eerie presence. But it is hard to say whether they are feeling the presence supernatural entity or are just uncomfortable with the simple knowledge of the countless deaths and suffering that occurred there.

Below: The Brooklyn Navy Yard. *Matt Zaller.*

Right: Fijian Chief Vendovi. *Archive.org.*

The U.S. Naval Hospital's cemetery is just a short stroll from the main building. Opened in 1831, this land once held up to 2,000 bodies. When the cemetery ran out of burial space in 1910, it was closed. Then in 1926, the bodies were exhumed and taken to Cypress Hill Cemetery (987 of them to be exact). The former cemetery was abandoned for almost ninety years. Then while digging around in 1997, workers came across human remains. An investigation was conducted with extensive research. After years of studying burial records and various maps, researchers concluded that while some bodies were relocated, more than half were left behind. In 2016, the land was officially transformed into the Naval Cemetery Landscape. This newly renovated cemetery is designed as a native plant pollinator meadow. Elevated walkways were placed throughout the park-like structure, so visitors won't have to step directly on the numerous, unaccounted-for graves. (It's possible they could even be walking over Chief Vendovi himself!)

18

WALLABOUT BAY

Wallabout Bay was first established in 1637, when a Dutchman named Jansen de Rapelje purchased the land from the Lenape tribe. To be exact, he purchased 335 acres of the bay's land. In 1801, the land was transformed into the Brooklyn Navy Yard, commissioned by John Adams. Yet it's what happened in between this land's purchase and the construction of the Brooklyn Navy Yard that caused Wallabout Bay to be the location of more deaths than all the battlefields in the Revolutionary War combined. More specifically, 8,000 Americans died in battle during the American Revolution, and 11,500 Americans died in Wallabout Bay.

Between 1776 and 1783, the British prison ship HMS *Jersey*, also known as "hell," was docked in New York Harbor during the Revolutionary War. Let's just say, dying on the *Titanic* was a more enjoyable experience than dying on this prison ship. If you don't believe me, hear it for yourself from survivor Robert Sheffield:

> *The heat was so intense that* [the three hundred–plus prisoners] *were all naked, which also served the well to get rid of vermin, but the sick were eaten up alive. Their sickly countenances and ghastly looks were truly horrible; some swearing and blaspheming; others crying, praying and wringing their hands; and stalking about like ghosts; others delirious, raving and storming, all panting for breath; some dead, and corrupting. The air was so foul that at times, a lamp could not be kept burning, by reason of which the bodies were not missed until they had been dead ten days. One person alone was admitted on deck at a time, after sunset, which occasioned much filth to run into the hold and mingle with the bilge water.* (Connecticut Gazette, *1778)*

The Brooklyn Navy Yard building. *Matt Zaller.*

The conditions on these ships were repugnant. Many prisoners died of disease and starvation. Most of their food (also known as "soup") was made using water from the East River, prepared in a copper pot, inadvertently poisoning them. Other food consumed on this ship consisted of spoiled mystery meat and moldy bread. Death was so habitual that every day, between five and ten bodies were thrown off the ship. For years, bones and skeletons washed up on the shores of the bay. (The remains were collected and eventually placed into a crypt called the Martyrs Monument, located in Fort Greene Park.)

All you had to do in order to land yourself onboard one of these ships was simply refuse to pledge allegiance to King George (or some other small infraction). Anyone and everyone was susceptible to this cruel and unusual punishment. Martin "Marty" Maher, the Brooklyn parks commissioner, stated, "Every man was offered freedom if he would swear to stop fighting. But there's no record that anyone took up the offer. No prisoner renounced the revolution to gain his freedom. Not one."

Following the construction of the Brooklyn Navy Yard, the docks would play a huge role in history, building some of the nation's most famous ships, including the USS *Missouri*, the USS *Monitor* and the USS *Arizona* (which sank in Pearl Harbor). By the time of World War II, 70,000 people were

Left: The interior of the old *Jersey* prison ship during the Revolutionary War. Engraving by Edward Bookhout, 1855. *Library of Congress.*

Below: A view of the Brooklyn Navy Yard in Wallabout Bay. *Matt Zaller.*

employed at the Brooklyn Navy Yard, including many women. However, that would all come to an end after a deadly fire broke out on December 19, 1960. While constructing the USS *Constellation*, a forklift damaged a fuel tank, spilling highly flammable liquid everywhere. The shipyard soon became engulfed in flames, leaving 50 people dead and 323 injured.

The Brooklyn Navy Yard was officially closed in 1966. Since then, it's become what some refer to as a "micro city." With more than 450 businesses and almost 11,000 employees, it has everything from rooftop farms (and wine vineyards) to a whiskey distillery.

PART X

PARK SLOPE

19

BOY WHO FELL FROM THE SKY

One of the worst plane crashes in history occurred at the intersection of Sterling Place and Seventh Avenue in Park Slope.

On December 16, 1960, a plane headed to Idlewild Airport (now John F. Kennedy International Airport) collided head-on with another plane headed to LaGuardia Airport, killing a total of 134 people—128 on board the aircraft and 6 on the ground. One of the planes landed on Staten Island, and the other plane crashed in the middle of Park Slope, setting fire to 10 brownstones, a funeral home, a deli and a laundromat. A church, ironically named the Pillar of Fire Church, was destroyed, killing its ninety-year-old caretaker.

There was only one survivor of the plane crash, an eleven-year-old boy named Stephen L. Boltz. Known as the "boy who fell from the sky," Stephen was your typical all-American sixth grader. He sang in the church choir, played on a Little League team and was an active Boy Scout. He dreamed of one day becoming an FBI agent. Stephen was flying from Chicago to New York to meet his mother and sister, who had flown in a day earlier, for Christmas. Stephen was originally supposed to be on their flight but stayed behind due to a sore throat. He flew alone the next day instead.

When the planes crashed, Stephen landed on a snowbank on the sidewalk, which civilians used to extinguish the flames. Still conscious and able to speak, he was more concerned with his mother who was waiting for him at the airport than his injuries, which included a broken leg. A woman named Dorothy M. Fletcher comforted Stephen and drove him to

The corner of Seventh Avenue and Sterling Place in Park Slope. *Matt Zaller.*

the hospital. On the way, he asked her if he was going to die. "Not if we can help it," she replied.

Stephen fought for his life for as long as he could while the world prayed for his recovery. On his hospital bed, he described the view of New York City from the airplane. "I remember looking out the plane window at the snow below covering the city. Then all of the sudden, there was an explosion.…I held onto my seat and then the plane crashed. It looked like a picture out of a fairy book. It was a beautiful sight." Unfortunately, Stephen passed away the next day from pneumonia; his lungs had been filled with jet fuel, resulting in pneumonia.

The Seventy-Eighth Police Precinct claims it is haunted by a little boy looking for his lost luggage, whom they believe is the ghost of Stephen. He is seen holding an airline ticket and sitting on the front steps of the building waiting. Psychics claim the spirit has told them that he knows first aid and can help the other injured passengers.

Evidence of the plane crash can still be seen around Park Slope. At 123 Sterling Place, the patched-up bricks are a different color from the rest of the building, as the original bricks were destroyed when the plane's twenty-five-foot-long right wing sliced through it. Another building in the neighborhood installed the remnants of the church's gates over its windows. This was also the first time a black box was used to investigate an accident.

20

PARK SLOPE ARMORY

One of the most famous landmarks in Brooklyn is the Park Slope Armory, also known as the Fourteenth Regiment Armory. Built between 1891 and 1895, this armory has reinvented itself more times than Madonna. In the past 130 years, it has served as a shooting range, a horse stable, a bowling alley, a practice space for the Dodgers, a skating rink, a sports arena, a YMCA, a women's homeless shelter and a storage space for the Macy's Thanksgiving Day Parade balloons.

Many movies have also been shot at the armory. *Meet Joe Black* was filmed inside, and the set built for Anthony Hopkins's lavish apartment had its very own indoor pool. Other films shot there have included *Raging Bull, Goodfellas, Donnie Brasco* and *Addicted to Love*. Inside the armory is a secret veteran's museum, filled with items from the Civil War to the Vietnam War. Another hidden treasure underneath the armory is a tunnel that leads out to the center of Prospect Park. Outside the armory is a stone from the battlefield of Gettysburg, which was bestowed on the city in 1894. And all over the armory are ghosts.

During a renovation in the 1950s, the armory's ghosts scared off some workers who were painting the interior. Suddenly, footprints began to appear all over the freshly painted ceiling and walls, which were rumored to have belonged to ghosts from the Spanish-American War.

Another notable ghost that haunts the building is the spirit of a Civil War veteran who once lived and worked there as an armorer. He'd spent his days protecting the ammunition and his nights inside his room, which was located in the armory's turret, where he would die in 1910 from natural causes. Some say his ghost still walks the halls, checking on the ammunition.

The Park Slope Armory. *Matt Zaller.*

21

LINCOLN PLAZA HOTEL

Let's take a peek inside one of Brooklyn's most notorious brothels, shall we? Now the location of luxury condos, 153 Lincoln Place used to be the neighborhood's house of ill repute.

The building was originally constructed in 1887 for the Pratt family, using the same architect who designed the Pratt Institute's campus. In the 1930s, the house was sold and turned into a home for unwed mothers. Then in the late 1940s, it was transformed into a hotel called Lincoln Plaza Hotel. The hotel was a hit and used as popular venue for special events and weddings—for a short while, at least.

As the years went by, the hotel's reputation declined. It was no secret what it had turned into. The clientele was, to put it frankly, sleazy. Rightfully so, this brothel upset the surrounding neighbors of the surrounding upscale Park Slope neighborhood.

In 2004, the *New York Times* published an article about the hotel's colorful history. The writer spoke to a man whose friend had tried to check into the hotel but was denied entry. "I think because he had luggage, they were convinced that he actually did want to check in," a dead giveaway for a pay-by-the-hour hotel. When he asked if there were any free rooms, the woman seated behind a large plexiglass window replied, "Not for you, sweetie."

The Lincoln Plaza Hotel was able to stay in business for all those decades because its employees were very well behaved. Even though everyone, including the police, knew what was going on inside the hotel's walls, there were never any complaints. They didn't make noise, they didn't allow people to loiter and they kept to themselves. In fact, they never had a single police record. That is until 1999, when a woman was found strangled to death in room 26.

The building was eventually sold and inevitably turned into luxury condominiums. For those in the know, however, it will always be known as the neighborhood hot-sheets hotel.

PART XI

PROSPECT PARK

22

123 ON THE PARK

Caledonian Hospital, built in 1910, treated Brooklynites for nearly one hundred years. It was eventually closed in 2003 and used as a set for *Law and Order*. Then in 2014, like most historic buildings, it was transformed into a luxury apartment complex called 123 on the Park.

Yet while the hospital rooms were renovated into bedrooms, the spirits of the hospital remained. Within six months of opening, three doormen quit on account of its ghosts. One doorman told the *Post* that the building is "a messed-up place to work because it's haunted." His daily security rounds in the basement included hearing the echoing of footsteps around surrounding him. Believing that he was being followed by an entity, he ran out.

Another doorman witnessed something supernatural. While looking at the security cameras, he watched as motion-sensor lights turned on in the stairwell, one by one, starting on the seventh floor and moving all the way down to the first floor. No one was there. Former doorman Robert Samuel claimed, "Just going down to the employees' locker room gave me an eerie feeling—like a sixth sense."

Residents at the building also claim to be haunted by former hospital patients. They've seen cabinets open and close, smelled strange odors lingering in the air, heard unexplained footsteps and watched lights switch on and off. A woman and her roommate, who wished to remain anonymous so that the ghosts wouldn't "come after" them, experienced multiple supernatural encounters in their apartment. As soon as they moved in, they would wake up in the middle of the night after hearing

123 on the Park. *Matt Zaller.*

noises coming from the kitchen, and saw their bedroom doors open and close. Others in the building have reported TVs turning on by themselves and objects flying off shelves.

The building itself quickly developed a reputation. According to the *New Yorker*, "A cab driver dropped one resident off with a warning: 'Be careful. It's full of skeletons.'" There was even a ghost hunter who came to inspect the building and saw a faint crucifix coming from the window.

Most people who find themselves living in a haunted apartment usually try to break their lease and move. Instead, the residents of 123 on the Park tried to use the ghosts to their advantage, citing that they should get a drop in their rent due to the phantoms. Unfortunately, the proposal was denied. They trying to use the spirits not only as a reason to not pay rent, but also as an excuse to not work out, as the gym was rumored to be located in the former morgue. As for the doormen, many claim the reason they have a high turnover rate is that the other buildings pay more.

23

LITCHFIELD VILLA

Before there was Prospect Park, there was Litchfield Villa. In fact, Prospect Park was literally built around Litchfield Villa. This Italianate-style mansion was constructed between 1855 and 1857 for Edwin C. Litchfield, where he lived with his wife and five children. Around this time, the spiritualism movement began to grow. Due to so many people dying suddenly in the Civil War, family and friends weren't able to say goodbye to their loved ones. Grieving and desperate, families turned to psychics and mediums for a chance to make contact with them. In fact, the spiritualism movement was so big that New York State created an entire town called Lily Dale, New York, in order to house the various clairvoyants. (The town still exists today, and residents are frequently tested to make sure they qualify to live there.)

In 1864, a woman named Margaret Cahill asked Litchfield if she could host a séance at his home in the hopes of communicating with her son, who had passed away in battle. He agreed, and the séance was held. Unfortunately, things went horribly wrong. At first, the lights began to flicker, and then plates started to break. Paintings fell off the walls, the table shook and gusts of wind swept through the room in a tornado-like manner. The air began to smell of sulfur, and the sound of grumbling could be heard. Then, all of a sudden, the room went dark. Two demons appeared with long red tongues and glowing green eyes. After a few seconds, they flew up through the ceiling up to the second floor. Everyone began to panic. One of the women fainted and fell to the floor, while others ran out of the house

Litchfield Villa. *Matt Zaller.*

Litchfield Villa's interior. *Courtesy of the Bob Levine Collection.*

screaming. One man almost got trampled by a horse carriage in his race to get away. Afterward, everything seemed to be back to normal—until the next night. The demons reappeared, only this time, they were in the upstairs window. These gargoyle-looking creatures, as they were described, are said to still be seen in the second-floor windows to this day.

Many rumors circulated about what exactly caused Litchfield Villa's demonic possession. The first theory was that the séance was done incorrectly, creating a vortex for demons to enter the home. The second theory was that Mrs. Cahill's son was in Hell, so by talking to him, it allowed demons to cross over. Lastly, it's said that a participant in the group was already possessed, and the séance released the demon from inside of her.

The scariest part of the séance is that every single person in attendance all died within the year. Mrs. Cahill and Mrs. Rossiter died from consumption; Mr. William Brownell died from the complications of an injury; Mr. George Vonderlin died from a "nervous attack"; and Mr. William Woodruff vanished completely, with many believing that he was taken to Hell by the devil himself. All historic records of him were erased.

Litchfield eventually donated the home to the park in 1868. Today, it is used by the parks department. Yet it still remains a popular location among mystics who perform rituals and séances, which are said to activate the demons.

24

QUAKER CEMETERY

Looking at a map of Prospect Park, you'll find everything from an ice-skating rink to a zoo. What you won't find, however, is a cemetery. But that doesn't mean there isn't one. In fact, there's quite a large one. Yet due to a number of spectators and gawkers, it's been erased from the guidebooks.

While Prospect Park was established in 1867, the Friends Cemetery was created seventeen years prior, with graves dating as far back as 1820. When

An 1870 Vaux and Olmsted map or plan of Prospect Park. *Source unknown.*

Top: Lawn tennis at Prospect Park. *Source unknown.*

Bottom: The Friends Cemetery in Prospect Park. *Matt Zaller.*

the land was being scouted for Prospect Park, the city realized that the cemetery was within the park's boundaries, so the park was built around it. Officially speaking, based on the number of headstones, there are 2,000 graves in the cemetery. However, Quakers didn't start using gravestones or markers until the 1850s, so historians believe there are actually around 3,500 bodies buried there.

A few notable people are buried inside the Friends Cemetery: former Brooklyn borough president Raymond Ingersoll, schoolteacher and activist Mary McDowell and, of course, Hollywood legend Montgomery Clift. This is where the trouble began. Clift was laid to rest in the Quaker cemetery per his mother's request in 1966. Since then, the once deliberately unassuming burial site has been swarmed with fans trying to get a glimpse of the actor's grave. The cemetery's sexton Bob Wilber relayed to the *New York Times* the constant trespassing of Clift fans whom he described as "people with purple hair and black T-shirts." In order to keep them out, barbed wire has been placed on top of a high fence surrounding the cemetery.

The cemetery is still active today and is used by the Quaker community.

PART XII

WILLIAMSBURG

Williamsburg Pizza. *Matt Zaller.*

25

BARCADE

Brooklyn, once dubbed "the city of churches" by the *Brooklyn Daily Eagle* in 1844, had more churches in all of New York City, most of which date to the nineteenth century. Along with these churches came the churches' graveyards. To break it down mathematically, more churches equal more graveyards. Many of these houses of worship were eventually closed and torn down, including the land that was reserved for the dead. As time went by and the neighborhoods began to grow, records and maps of these churches were lost. This resulted in many houses, bars, restaurants, et cetera being built over former cemeteries—many of which were still full.

One such building is located on Union Avenue, across from the famous Kellogg's Diner. This abandoned and forgotten cemetery belonged to the Old Methodist Burying Ground. Built in 1835, it was used as a graveyard until it closed in 1856. Some of the bodies were exhumed and moved to Cyprus Hills Cemetery, but many were left behind (a pattern you've probably noticed by now). This particular cemetery held more than thirty thousand bodies, perhaps the reason many bodies were left behind.

The relocation of bodies upset the families of the deceased. In 1893, the *New York Times* wrote an article about the public's reaction to moving the corpses. When the writer was interviewing the chief of the malcontents, he said, "Fudge! They are only bones, so much rotten old bones! I don't care a fillip about them! What I want to know is whether there will be a surplus of cash after the removals are made and whether it will be divided among the plot holders." By 1860, the land was converted for residential use.

Barcade. *Matt Zaller.*

Today, the location of the Old Methodist Burying Ground is now home to Barcade, a bar filled with arcade games. While some bartenders are convinced that there is something supernatural going on, Paul Kermizian, who opened Barcade in 2004, says, "The only ghosts we've seen have been in our Ms. Pac Man game!"

26

THE CHARLESTON

W hen you first step off the L train at Bedford Avenue, you'll come face to face with the Charleston. While it doesn't look like much, you will notice that its outside tables are always occupied, even during the daytime. Inside, the wooden bar, sticky to the touch, leads to a couple of Skee-Ball games. It's also one of the oldest bars in Brooklyn, having opened nearly a century ago, in 1933. Like New York City cockroaches, the Charleston has withstood the test of time. The fact that patrons get a free pizza with the purchase of beer may have also helped play a role in this dive bar's sustainability.

The Charleston.
Matt Zaller.

Like most other structures in this neighborhood, the Charleston was originally built as a boardinghouse in the nineteenth century. These housing units were mostly filled with working-class immigrants, who were employed by the surrounding factories. One particular tenant was a fifty-three-year-old widow who lived there in 1889. She was a single mother and unemployed, despite her best efforts to find work. One day while her son was at school, she hanged herself in the building's ceiling, telling others that she was "tired of this world."

That was not the only (reported) death that occurred in the building. In June 2015, a thirty-two-year-old man was found beaten and unconscious outside of the bar after he had gotten into a fight. The man sustained severe head injuries and was taken to Bellevue Hospital. He was declared brain dead and taken off life support a few days later.

27

McCARREN PARK POOL

Let's face it. There are two kinds of pools—no, not outdoor or indoor—private or public. Unlike private pools, public pools come with their unique set of eccentricities. Let's investigate a perfect example: McCarren Park Pool.

The McCarren Park Pool was created in 1936 by Parks Commissioner Robert Moses as part of the New Deal. The pool is so enormous that it can fit four Olympic-sized pools inside of it and has a capacity of 6,800 people. The pool quickly became a popular destination for Williamsburg and Greenpoint residents looking to cool off in the summer heat. However, as the years went by, it began to lose its charm and fell into despair. By the 1980s, it was borderline dangerous. A woman named Jenifer Badamo, a lifelong resident of the neighborhood, was barred by her mother from going to the pool because it was "a horror show." The pool was eventually closed in 1984 for repairs, yet it would be twenty-eight years before those repairs were actually done.

Within that time, the empty pool became a mecca for drugs and crime. The homeless community soon took up residence, and many of them died there. In 2008, park workers went to investigate "a foul odor coming from a shed at the pool for months." When they entered the pool shed, they discovered a body so badly decomposed that its age, sex and race were completely undetectable. However, that was hardly the first death that occurred there.

There have been at least five people who were rumored to have drowned/died in the pool. The most notable was a little girl who drowned in the

McCarren Park Pool at night. *Matt Zaller.*

McCarren Park in 1937. *Source unknown.*

1930s, as well as a fourteen-year-old boy who drowned there in 1977. There are also rumors that two men drowned during a midnight swim and that another was murdered.

It should come as no surprise that the pool is famously haunted. Many ghost hunters and paranormal investigators have visited in the hopes of making contact with its ghosts. The most active spirit is that of the little girl who drowned. People have seen her calling out for help and have felt cold chills in her presence. The ghost of the little boy can also be seen; only in his case, witnesses experience warm spots. Evidence of drops in temperature, orbs and disembodied voices have also been recorded. Even dogs have responded to the paranormal activity. When they approach the pool area, they begin to freak out and pull in the opposite direction.

The pool was eventually reopened in 2012, after an almost thirty-year hiatus and a $50 million renovation. It wouldn't be long before trouble ensued. On its very first day it opened, the pool was closed an hour early due to rioting and assault. A group of teens attacked a lifeguard, causing him to almost drown. A few days later, three men were arrested after punching a police officer in the face and wounding another. What instigated these attacks? They were told not to do any backflips into the pool.

That wasn't the worst part. Due to a lack of bathrooms, the streets were covered in feces and urine. According to the *New York Times*, "Nearby merchants complained that pool visitors tossed litter on the ground, tagged buildings with graffiti and relieved themselves in public." One of those merchants, Meredith Chesney, revealed that someone had not only graffitied her storefront but also defecated in front of it.

28

MOST HOLY TRINITY CHURCH

Located in Williamsburg, Most Holy Trinity Church dates to the 1880s. It was even written about in *A Tree Grows in Brooklyn*, in which it was described as the "most beautiful church in Brooklyn." Mysterious tunnels, hallways, fake closets and secret passages are said to span the building. (It's even said they were used as a part of the Underground Railroad.)

Most Holy Trinity Church was built on hallowed ground—yes, the church was built on top of a cemetery. Well, it was a *former* cemetery, used from 1841 to 1853. The cemetery's bodies were supposed to be relocated, but alas, they were not. Rumors quickly spread that their ghosts were haunting the property, upset at their remains' treatment. More specifically, it is said that the church's school is haunted by them. Claims of hearing footsteps pacing back and forth have been reported throughout the building, and lights have been seen flickering on and off in the gymnasium.

In the church's rectory, a pastor died in his room on the second floor in 1895. (He and his predecessor are both buried in the church's crypt.) Since then, it's rumored that the area is haunted. Due to this stigma, residents refuse to sleep in there, so it has been designated as a guest room. People who have stayed in the room claim to have been woken up by footsteps walking around and other unexplained noises. The kitchen staircase is also home to some paranormal activity, and dogs often stare (no pun intended) at it in a hypnotic-like trance.

Aside from its rich history and ornate architecture, Most Holy Trinity Church is known for a gruesome murder that took place there on August 29,

Most Holy Trinity Church. *Matt Zaller.*

Left: Most Holy Trinity Church. *Source unknown.*

Right: The church's second pastor, Monsignor Michael May, built its rectory in 1872. *Source unknown.*

1897. A man named George Steltz was bludgeoned to death when he walked in on two men robbing the poor box. Steltz, who worked at the church as a parish sexton and a bell ringer, was an avid member of the congregation. According to the *Travel Channel*, his bloody handprint will appear from time to time on the staircase leading up to the bell tower. His name can also be seen on a stained-glass window, which he had donated to the church twelve years prior to his death. Phantom bells go off at unexplained times, which people believe to be Steltz. One of the men who murdered Steltz, a fellow parishioner of the church, was eventually executed for another murder, but the other culprit was never found. People believe that Steltz's spirit will continue to haunt the church until his murder has been solved.

ST. MAZIE'S

St. Mazie Bar and Supper Club is an ideal spot for a date night. Its cocktails are creative, the lighting is heavily luminated via candlelight and, if you're lucky, you'll catch a live jazz show.

During Prohibition, there were more speakeasies in Brooklyn than there were in any other place in New York City (estimated at around one hundred thousand). And it is because of this that Brooklyn was dubbed the "wettest borough." St. Mazie was one of these speakeasies. Not only was it an illegal bar, but the basement served as a gambling den. With its rich history of crime, it's no wonder that it is now rumored to be haunted.

St. Mazie's. *Matt Zaller.*

Servers and staff claim that chairs and glasses move on their own, along with the usual unexplained noises. During an interview with the band Blonde Redhead, frequent St. Mazie patron and singer Kazu Makino told *Bedford + Bowery*, "Apparently, it's a bit haunted here. Vanessa was telling us about this, and then it happened right in front of us. The girl who was closing the bar was freaking out. This candle basically flew off the wall. It was so bizarre."

SWEETWATER

When walking into Sweetwater, it feels as if you've been transported back in time. The tin ceilings and dark wood allow for a nostalgic glimpse into what a Williamsburg restaurant would have looked like one hundred years ago.

The building itself was originally constructed in 1899 as a boardinghouse. In 1924, it was bought by Charles Szyjka and his family, who transformed it into a restaurant with upstairs apartments. The Szyjka family would live, work and die there. The first death occurred in the apartments upstairs. Charles's wife, Katherine, died while giving birth to their daughter, Anna. After her death, Charles would marry a woman named Eva, who also happened to be Katherine's younger sister. But she, too, would succumb to the same fate, passing away while giving birth, this time to a son named Michael. Charles, along with his third wife, Jennie, continued to run the restaurant and occupy the upstairs apartments for almost three decades. When Mr. Szyjka died in 1955, his daughter Anna took over the business.

Anna was a beloved staple in the community. She frequented several churches and went out of her way to help feed local workers. She successfully kept the restaurant running for the next fifteen years until she had no choice but to close. By the 1970s, Williamsburg had become rundown and desolate. What was once a thriving and busy area was then empty and vandalized. Crime in the area increased rapidly, and Anna was frequently robbed. However, she remained there. In fact, for a time, she was the only person who lived on the street. Anna eventually moved to Manhattan at the insistence

Sweetwater. *Matt Zaller.*

of her family, but she swore that she would one day return to her home in Williamsburg. Unfortunately, Anna passed away in 2003 before she had a chance to return.

The next year, Sweetwater was opened. By this time, the gentrification of Williamsburg had begun. Artists moved in, and the once shuttered storefronts were then occupied with coffee shops and mom-and-pop stores.* Abandoned warehouses were turned into upscale lofts and the boardinghouses into themed dive bars—a far cry from their blue-collar past life. Needless to say, Sweetwater was an instant hit. This gastropub provided the perfect space for an after-work drink or a first date. Once again, the building was a beloved neighborhood eatery.

One day, a porter decided to rest his eyes and went to the basement for a nap. When he woke up, he saw "the devil" standing over him. He immediately quit. Then came the second porter, Miguel Vargas. Only this time, instead of seeing the devil, he saw a ghost. While opening the restaurant one morning, Vargas came face to face with an apparition of a woman. She wore an ornate white dress and had silver hair. She was in her forties and looked as if she was from a different era. To his surprise, she appeared more like a regular person than a ghost. He watched as she walked across the dining room to the basement before vanishing. Much like his successor, Vargas ran out in fear.

Vargas wasn't alone. His coworkers also reported having supernatural experiences. Some claimed to feel as if someone was watching them. Others said lights would go on and off. There was even a "glow" that came from the basement. But the most common phenomenon was unexplained music. And it is because of this that the ghost is believed to be none other than Anna (according to her family).

As Sweetwater neared its tenth anniversary, its owners began to do some construction. In order to bolster the restaurant's support beams, they had to dig up the floors. That's when they discovered a burial site. Yes, you read that right—a burial site. In it they found a gold ring, a small stone Madonna and a child figure, children's shoes and animal bones. While they reburied most of the items, including the shoes and bones, they kept a few—a gold ring and the Madonna statue—which they displayed on the bar. Then bizarre things started happening.

First were the glasses. One by one, they all started breaking. If they weren't broken, they would crack. If they were held, they would shatter. If they were on the shelf, they would fall down. This resulted in up to twenty broken glasses a day. Some believed it was the cause of ghosts, while others believed it was due to construction nearby.

After the *New York Times* published an article about Sweetwater's hauntings in 2014, "ghost hunters" would often show up in the hope of investigating. Maybe the hauntings are simply Anna letting everyone know that she finally made it back to 105 North Sixth Street after all.

---

* Today it's all large cooperations, as the rent is too high for smaller businesses. One store's rent went up by 44 percent. When they first opened in 2008, it was $8,625 per month. A decade later, it was $26,000.

PART XIII

~~

ASSORTED MORBID

BOOS AND BOOZE

In the 1920s, America voted to make liquor illegal. This time in history was known as Prohibition.

The rich could still buy bootlegged liquor but for a high price. The poor could not. Unable to afford the real thing, they decided to make their own. However, this moonshine came at its own price.

Figuring that any organic material could be distilled, wood seemed like the easiest choice. Poor people began to distill sawdust and even their own furniture. The only problem was that when wood was distilled, it produced methanol. Once ingested, the body breaks it down, creating formaldehyde, a highly deadly and poisonous chemical. This resulted in consumers' blurred vision, hallucinations, paralysis and death. By 1925 alone, 4,154 people had died from drinking wood alcohol.

The government began to deliberately add even more chemicals and poisons to over-the-counter methanol in order to discourage people from consuming the toxic moonshine. They even put labels on the bottles promising blindness after the third glass. Unfortunately, this only made things worse, resulting in over ten thousand deaths.

Poisonous alcohol wasn't the only deadly thing that came from Prohibition. Crime rates soared, as people saw new opportunities in the demand for bootlegged liquor. Some of the top bootleggers made over $60 million a year selling booze. The most prominent figures in the bootlegging industry were Al Capone, Meyer Lansky, Bugsy Siegel, Johnny Torrio and Lucky Luciano. They ran out of Brooklyn and were famously dubbed "Murder Inc." They lived up to their name, too, being responsible for over one thousand brutal murders.

TAPHOPHOBIA

Taphophobia: the fear of being buried alive. We all have this tiny irrational fear tucked away in the back of our minds. It's the same level of fear we have of being eaten by sharks while sitting on dry land. However, there was a time in history when this fear wasn't so ludicrous. In fact, it was more rational to have it than to not.

Before modern technology, there was no reliable way to determine if someone was dead. Of course, there were clues and tell-tale signs. Simply looking dead was one of them. This was a very faulty system considering that many of these people were actually in a coma. Diseases such as yellow fever, cholera and tuberculosis spread like wildfire throughout towns and cities, wreaking havoc. Many of their victims were left in comatose states, leading others to believe they were deceased. In fact, by the turn of the century, it was believed that one person per week was accidentally buried alive.

So, how do we know so many people were buried alive? Bodies were constantly being exhumed from the ground. This was mostly due to grave robbers stealing jewelry off the bodies and doctors stealing corpses for their medical students. These cadavers were so valuable that you could pay your entire college tuition with one of them in 1700s Scotland. Body snatchers, also known as "resurrectionists," had multiple ways of collecting the corpses. Aside from merely digging them up, they would obtain them by bribing undertakers and churches. This occasionally led to "resurrection riots," in which fights between the body snatchers and the public broke.

A shocking revelation and grim pattern started to occur. When the coffins were opened, people noticed scratch marks all over the lid. They soon realized that people were being buried alive. Panic escalated. In order to

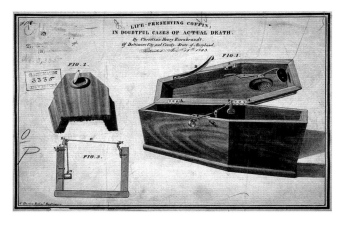

A safety coffin patent from 1845. *Model by Christian Eisenbrandt, public domain.*

prevent these premature burials, "safety coffins" were invented. For example, one safety coffin had a "straw" that could allow someone to breathe while they waited for help. Others had a window in through which a person could wave. However, the most famous of all was the bell ringer coffin. A string was attached to the corpse's finger, leading up to the ground with a bell attached at the end of it. The thought process behind this was that if a person were to wake up, their fingers would move, setting off the bell. These "dead ringers" would be literally saved by the bell. Due to the fact that these bells could go off at any hour, someone had to wait in the cemetery overnight. This is where we get the term "graveyard shift."

Needless to say, none of these safety coffins ever worked. In Germany, "waiting mortuaries" were created. There, naked bodies of the (possibly) recently deceased were placed on tables and examined. Tests were then performed on them to see if the person was still alive. These tests included slicing the soles of their feet with razor blades, cutting off their fingers, burning their noses, putting beetles in their ears, giving them tobacco enemas (or "blowing smoke up their rear"), pouring boiling water on them and even pulling their tongue back and forth for hours. Fortunately, by the turn of the century, modern instruments, such as the stethoscope, helped determine someone's fate quickly and easily.

Before funeral parlors came into practice, bodies would remain in the home while the family made the funeral arrangements. During this time, family and friends would come to pay their respects. This is believed to be the inspiration for what we now call "wakes." Rumor has it that during this time, the mourners would wait by the body late at night to see if they'd "wake up." While some may argue that this is just a myth, the practice of waiting up to eight days for a body to wake up has been used since ancient

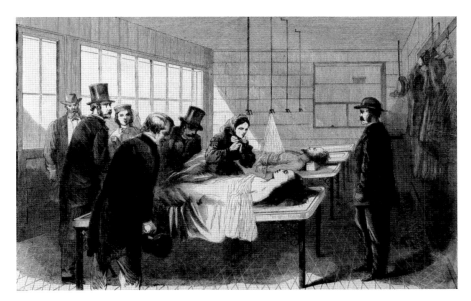

Visiting a body inside a waiting mortuary. *From Wikimedia.*

times. The deceased loved ones were displayed in the home's parlor, which was also referred to as the "death room." By the 1930s, funeral homes had become the norm, and the practice of home wakes was discontinued. In an effort to reinvent the parlor, the *Ladies Home Journal* changed its name from the "death room" to the "living room."

In May 2022, a man in Shanghai was declared dead and taken to a funeral home. When workers opened the body bag, it was discovered that he was still alive.

MORBID FACTS

How Many Types of Hauntings Are There?

There are four types of hauntings: residual, intelligent, poltergeist and demonic possession. Residual hauntings are usually the result of a traumatic event or sudden death. Due to this, a residual ghost will continue to reenact the events. These ghosts don't realize they are dead. If you've ever seen a ghost walk through a wall, that's because that wall did not exist when the ghost was alive; therefore, they don't see it (or you). Intelligent hauntings are the exact opposite. These ghosts are aware they are dead and are able to communicate with you, which they can do by moving objects. Next up is a poltergeist haunting. *Poltergeist* is a German word that means "noisy ghost." Poltergeists can either be playful or malicious and aim to cause disturbances. Signs of poltergeists include moving objects, electrical interferences and physical attacks. Reports of poltergeist activity dates to the first century. Demonic possessions occur when a demon or a spirit takes over a person's soul. They are also synonymous with Ouija boards. When one of these possessions occur, it takes an exorcism being performed to get rid of them. The first exorcism was performed more than four thousand years ago in Mesopotamia, and the Vatican even issued official guidelines on how to perform them in 1614.

The Devil's Hour

Also referred to as the "witching hour," this is the time of night between 3:00 and 4:00 a.m. It is believed that this is when supernatural entities are at their strongest. One of the reasons for this belief is that Jesus was executed at 3:00 p.m., making 3:00 a.m. the opposite. Something extra spooky is that most people who die in their sleep do so between the hours of 3:00 and 4:00 a.m.

How Much Does the Human Soul Weigh?

In 1907, a doctor named Duncan Macdougall weighed six terminally ill patients right before they died and at the moment of death. All six patients lost an average of twenty-one grams. He did the experiment once more, only this time, he used fifteen dying dogs. When none of the dogs lost any weight, it was "scientifically concluded" that dogs have no souls. (Clearly, his scale must have been broken.)

How Much Does the Human Soul Cost?

Starting from the 1600s through the 1800s, people in Great Britain could pawn their souls for money. These "sin eaters" were hired to absorb a deceased person's misdeeds by eating bread that had been placed on the corpse's face or chest. The price tag for a soul? A few bucks and a pastry.

Smells Like Death

Back in the days before embalming (which was invented by a Brooklynite), bodies would start to decompose in the days leading up to the funeral. Flowers were sent to help mask the smell. On a similar note, the snapdragon flower turns into the shape of skulls when it dries out. Spooky potpourri, anyone?

Tastes Like Death

In 1946, after a botched execution via an electric chair (nicknamed "Gruesome Gertie"), Willie Francis survived. When he was asked what it felt like to survive being exhausted, he described death as "tasting like cold peanut butter."

WHICH WINDOW? WITCH WINDOW!

Native to the state of Vermont, these forty-five-degree-angle windows date to the 1830s. Superstition ran rampant in New England at this time. The theory behind this is that people believed witches were not able to enter homes via a tilted window, due to the fact that their broomstick would not be able to fit.

CIRCLE BARNS

If you've ever driven through New England, you may have noticed circular-shaped barns. This design was originated in 1826 by the Shakers in Massachusetts, who believed that if there were no corners, there would be no place for the devil to hide. Makes sense.

YOU HAIN'T COMING IN HERE!

Haint Blue is a light bluish-green color that is often painted on porch ceilings throughout the Deep South. The term *haint* comes from the southern word for "haunt." It is believed that this color scares away ghosts (also known as "haints") by tricking them into thinking the ceiling is water (which they cannot cross). Another thought is that the blue reminds ghosts of heaven, making them want to go up instead of inside the home. The color is also said to keep away mosquitos, which caused thousands of deaths by spreading yellow fever and disease for centuries.

HALLOWEEN'S HOMETOWN

Ireland! Dating back two thousand years, Halloween is derived from Samhain (*sam*, or "summer," and *fuin*, or "end"). This Celtic festival celebrated the changing of seasons, which was said to be the time of year when spirits are most active. People wore masks so that the dead would not recognize them (especially those whom the spirits disliked while alive). Large bonfires were built, and turnips were carved in order to scare them off. (This is where the tradition of carving pumpkins comes from.)

Who Is Michael Myers Face Based On?

The answer is: William Shatner! The budget for the film was so low that they had to purchase the cheapest mask possible, which, for less than two dollars, belonged to Captain Kirk. They turned the mask inside out, painted it white, removed the facial hair and cut out the eyes.

FYI: This House Is Haunted

In all fifty states, there is only one in which you must legally disclose if your property is haunted before selling it. And that state is our very own New York. It is a legal obligation in the state of New York to let the buyer know beforehand that there may be a ghost in the home. Known as the "Ghostbusters Ruling," this law came into action after a man in Nyack, New York, purchased a house he didn't know was haunted (even though it was literally a stop on a ghost tour). The case was taken to the supreme court, officially making it the only "legally haunted house" in the country.

Triskaidekaphobia

Triskaidekaphobia is the fear of the number thirteen. Here in New York City, 91 percent of buildings do not have a thirteenth floor. Instead, it's either relabeled as 12B or 14. (In China, it's the fourth floor that is skipped.)

Serial Killers Statistics

You need to kill at least three people to qualify as a serial killer (with a "resting period" in between murders). Ted Bundy once worked for a suicide hotline. Most serial killers are born in November. Left-handed people are more likely to become serial killers (à la Jack the Ripper). There are currently twenty-five to fifty active serial killers in the United States with a 40 percent chance of not getting caught.

VAMPIRES IN BROOKLYN

Every year, New Yorkers bite ten times more people than sharks do worldwide. In 2020, there were 129 shark attacks reported compared to 1,600 reports of New Yorkers biting each other.

WHY DO WE SAY BLESS YOU AFTER SOMEONE SNEEZES?

It all started in the year 519. Sneezing was the very first sign of the plague, so Pope Gregory I ordered everyone to immediately bless any person who sneezed by saying "God bless you." Basically, it was an instant prayer. This is also why we say "goodbye," which is short for "God be with ye." Another reason comes from superstition. It was believed that when a person sneezed, their heart would stop, giving the devil a chance to capture their soul. Others believed that sneezing was your body's way of forcing out an invading spirit. "God bless you" was said as protection.

SOS

If you've ever been on a cruise and heard the term "operation white star" from someone's walkie-talkie as you made your way through an all-you-can-eat buffet, that means someone on the ship has just died. This doesn't call for a burial at sea, but it does call for being zipped up in a bag and taken to the ship's morgue. (All cruise ships have morgues, nicknamed the "coffin locker," big enough to store three to four people.) Unfortunately, there have been times when the body count has exceeded the morgue's capacity. In these cases, bodies are taken to the *food* freezer. The good news is that the cost of storing and transporting the body is usually covered by travel insurance.

COTARD'S SYNDROME

Dating back to 1882, this condition is when someone thinks they are dead or do not exist. This disorder is also referred to as walking corpse syndrome, which can result in them not eating or speaking. That's one excuse for not paying taxes!

The Creepiest Place on Earth!

Disney World is said to be the most haunted place in the world. Thousands of people walk through it every day, making memories that last a lifetime. And it is because of this that so many people want to stay forever. Family and friends scatter the ashes of their loved ones throughout the amusement park, which they had to create a special codeword for whenever they needed to vacuum them up. This code is called a "HEPA cleanup," which occurs about once a month. The most popular spot for spreading loved one's ashes is the Haunted Mansion.

Debunking Ghost Sightings

I hate to say this—I really do—but if you see a ghost, it's probably a side effect of an "environmental phenomenon or physiological condition, such as sleep paralysis and the hypnogogic and hypnopompic hallucinations that accompany it," according Joe Nickel, who has been studying the paranormal for over forty years. And the most common cause of seeing ghosts? Carbon monoxide poisoning.

BIBLIOGRAPHY

1. Construction and Destruction

Broyles, Susannah. "The Curse of the Roeblings? The Construction of the Brooklyn Bridge." Museum of the City of New York. September 11, 2012. https://blog.mcny.org/2012/09/11/the-curse-of-the-roeblings-the-construction-of-the-brooklyn-bridge.

Klein, Christopher. "Construction of the Brooklyn Bridge Took 14 Years—And Multiple Lives." History. May 21, 2021. https://www.history.com/news/brooklyn-bridge-construction-deaths.

Watson, Bruce. "Why There's No Way Brooklyn Bridge Will Be Better than the Brooklyn Bridge." *Esquire*, February 5, 2014. https://www.esquire.com/entertainment/movies/news/a27227/brooklyn-bridge-bridge-of-death-esq-0214/.

2. Alien Abductions

Booth, Billy John. "Abduction in Manhattan." Appalachian Ghost Walks. https://www.appalachianghostwalks.com/USUFOCenter/ufologist/booth/manhattan1.html.

Hopkins, Budd. "Witnessed: The True Story of the Brooklyn Bridge UFO Abductions." Brooklyn Library. https://www.bklynlibrary.org/item?b=10532571.

3. Deadly Scream

Frishberg, Hannah. "'The Bridge Is Falling': The Story of the Brooklyn Bridge's Deadly Stampede." Brownstoner. June 21, 2016. https://www.brownstoner.com/history/brooklyn-bridge-death-stampede-tragedy-1883/.

Gannon, Devin. "One Week After the Brooklyn Bridge Opened, a Rumor of its Collapse Caused a Fatal Stampede." 6sqft. May 30, 2018. https://www.6sqft.com/one-week-after-the-brooklyn-bridge-opened-a-rumor-of-its-collapse-caused-a-fatal-stampede/.

McNamara, Robert. "Brooklyn Bridge Disaster." Thought Co. November 19, 2018. https://www.thoughtco.com/brooklyn-bridge-disaster-1773696.

Wallache, Alex. "Rumor of Brooklyn Bridge Collapse Sparked Fatal Stampede During Opening Week." Untapped Cities. October 23. 2013. https://untappedcities.com/2013/10/23/rumor-brooklyn-bridge-stampede-collapse-sparked-fatal-during-opening-week/.

4. Brooklyn Bridge Boos

Raquel Laneri, Hana R. Alberts and Riedel Michael. "New York City's Most Haunted Spots Will Terrify You." *New York Post*, October 28, 2017. https://nypost.com/2017/10/28/nycs-most-haunted-spots-will-terrify-you/https://discover.hubpages.com/religion-philosophy/The-Haunted-Brooklyn-Bridge.

5. Ice Cream Fires

"Brooklyn Waterfront History. Fire!" https://www.bkwaterfronthistory.org/story/fire/.

Tracy, Thomas. "Man, 86, Killed in Boat Fire Near Brooklyn Bridge Park." *NY Daily News*, January 9, 2021. https://www.nydailynews.com/new-york/nyc-crime/ny-nyc-boat-fire-man-dead-20210109-vanvhcz7tfe2le53wxibxula2q-story.html.

6. Lefferts-Laidlaw House

Scout. "The Haunting of 136 Clinton Avenue (From the NY Times!)." Scouting New York. October 20, 2010. http://www.scoutingny.com/halloween-in-ny-the-haunting-of-136-clinton-avenue-as-reported-in-the-ny-times/.

7. H.P. Lovecraft's Brooklyn

Bowery Boys. "H.P. Lovecraft's Very Bizarre Hatred of Red Hook and Brooklyn Heights." August 20, 2015. https://www.boweryboyshistory.com/2015/08/h-p-lovecrafts-very-bizarre-hatred-of-red-hook-brooklyn.html.

Getlen, Larry. "Ghost Story." *New York Post*, August 14, 2008. https://nypost.com/2008/08/14/ghost-story/.

Poets & Writers. "H.P. Lovecraft's Brooklyn Heights Home." https://www.pw.org/literary_places/hp_lovecrafts_home_169_clinton_street.

8. Tavern in the Woods

Bowery Boys. "A Brooklyn Ghost Story: A Famous Actress, A Rowdy Tavern, Cobble Hill's 'Ghost-Haunted Spot' and a Fool Named Boerum." March 21, 2013. https://www.boweryboyshistory.com/2013/03/a-brooklyn-ghost-story-famous-actress.html.

Dixon Leasing. "10 of the Best Local Haunted Houses & Spooktacular Ghost Stories." https://www.dixonleasing.com/blog/neighborhood-expert/10-of-the-best-local-haunted-houses-spooktacular-ghost-stories.

Musings and Adventures. "10+ Haunted Brooklyn Places & Spooky Stories." September 7, 2020. https://musingsandadventures.com/2020/09/07/brooklyn-haunted-spots-spirits-spooky-stories/.

Stiles, Henry Reed. "History of the City of Brooklyn, Vol. 2." 1869. https://books.google.com/books?id=p3MxAAAAMAAJ&pg=PA346&dq=%22sweede%27s+fly%22+brooklyn&hl=en&sa=X&ei=oyFLUa3mCajJ0QGGqmIFQ#v=onepage&q=boerum&f=false.

Wikipedia. "Boerum Hill." https://en.wikipedia.org/wiki/Boerum_Hill.

9. Tunnel to Nowhere

Dylan. "Atlantic Ave. Tunnel." Atlas Obscura. February 10, 2010. https://www.atlasobscura.com/places/atlantic-avenue-tunnel.

Seymour, Ann. "The Light at the End of the Tunnel that Never Goes Out." Bklyner. October 2, 2018. https://bklyner.com/the-light-at-the-end-of-the-tunnel-that-never-goes-out/.

Wikipedia. "Cobble Hill Tunnel." https://en.wikipedia.org/wiki/Cobble_Hill_Tunnel.

10. Freakshows and Frights

Button, Rachel. "17 Weird Things About Coney Island We Didn't Know (8 We Didn't Want To)." The Travel. December 25, 2018. https://www.thetravel.com/weird-things-about-coney-island/.

Haunted Places. "Haunted Places in Coney Island, New York." https://www.hauntedplaces.org/coney-island-ny/.

Miss Cellania. "Coney Island Freaks of Yesterday and Today." Mental Floss. February 14, 2008. https://www.mentalfloss.com/article/18052/coney-island-freaks-yesterday-and-today.

Prakash, Alisha. "Coney Island Once Had an Elephant-Shaped Brothel… Plus 10 Other Ridiculous Facts About the 'Hood.'" Thrillist. June 15, 2016. https://www.thrillist.com/lifestyle/new-york/weird-facts-you-didnt-know-about-coney-island.

Robinson, Julian. "The Horrifying Human Zoos: Shocking Photos Reveal How Zoos Around the World Kept 'Primitive Natives' in Enclosures as Westerners Gawped and Jeered at Them Just 60 Years Ago." *Daily Mail*, March 17, 2017. https://www.dailymail.co.uk/news/article-4323366/Photos-reveal-horrifying-human-zoos-early-1900s.html.

Smith, Peter. "The Stunt that Launched Nathan's Famous Stand on Coney Island." Smithsonian. July 3, 2012. https://www.smithsonianmag.com/arts-culture/the-stunt-that-launched-nathans-famous-stand-on-coney-island-312344/.

Wikipedia. "Circus Sideshow." https://en.wikipedia.org/wiki/World_Circus_Sideshow.

11. Brooklyn Theater Fire

Britton, Joshua. "Tragedy, Welfare, and Reform: The Impact of the Brooklyn Theater Fire of 1876." Common Place. 2013. http://commonplace.online/article/tragedy-welfare-reform/.

History. "Hundreds Die in Brooklyn Theater Fire." November 13, 2009. https://www.history.com/this-day-in-history/hundreds-die-in-brooklyn-theater-fire.

Journal of the Bizarre. "Haunted Brooklyn: The Great Theatre Fire of 1876." March 15, 2016. http://www.bizarrejournal.com/2016/03/haunted-brooklyn-great-theatre-fire-of.html.

Wikipedia. "Brooklyn Theatre Fire." https://en.wikipedia.org/wiki/Brooklyn_Theatre_fire

12. High School Haunts

New York Times. "Boy Hurt in High School Fight Dies; Had Been Unable to Speak Since Bout." January 7, 1922. https://www.nytimes.com/1922/01/07/archives/boy-hurt-in-high-school-fight-dies-had-been-unable-to-speak-since.html.

Parascandola, Rocco, Mark Morales, Erin Durkin and Helen Kennedy. "Brooklyn Teen Stabbed with Scissors Over Hoops Game." *New York Daily News*, December 20, 2011. https://www.nydailynews.com/new-york/brooklyn/brooklyn-teen-stabs-fellow-student-stollen-basketball-erasmus-hall-high-school-article-1.994507.

Wikipedia. "Erasmus Hall High School." https://en.wikipedia.org/wiki/Erasmus_Hall_High_School.

Young, Michelle. "The Abandoned School Inside Erasmus Hall in Flatbush, Brooklyn and the Stained Glass Gems in the School Complex." Untapped Cities. June 23, 2017. https://untappedcities.com/2017/06/23/the-abandoned-school-inside-erasmus-hall-in-flatbush-brooklyn-and-the-stained-glass-gems-in-the-school-complex/.

13. Melrose Park

Brooklyn Daily Eagle. "The Ghost Story of the Mansion in Melrose Park." June 22, 1884. http://bklyn-genealogy-info.stevemorse.org/Town/1884.MansionMelrosePk.html.

———. "The Haunting of Melrose Hall." October 13, 1895. https://freakyfolktales.wordpress.com/the-haunting-of-melrose-hall-a-ghost-story-of-the-american-revolution/.

Queens College. "Hidden NYC Haunted Sites You may not of Heard Of." http://qcvoices.qwriting.qc.cuny.edu/treasan/2016/10/25/hidden-nyc-haunted-sites-you-may-not-of-heard-of/.

14. Bodies of Water

Albrecht, Leslie. "Sludgie the Whale Visited the Gowanus Canal 10 Years Ago Today." DNAinfo. April 17, 2017. https://www.dnainfo.com/new-york/20170417/gowanus/sludgie-whale-gowanus-canal/.

Ample Hills. "It Came from Gowanus." https://amplehills.com/flavors/it-came-from-gowanus.

Bonanos, Christopher. "A Brief History of Slime." *New York Magazine*, July 10, 2009. https://nymag.com/news/intelligencer/topic/57886/.

Hynes, Thomas. "Aw Shucks: The Tragic History of New York City Oysters." Untapped Cities. February 3, 2021. https://untappedcities.com/2021/02/03/history-new-york-city-oysters/.

Pardon Me for Asking. "The Tale of a Whale Hunt in the Gowanus Canal…in 1928." November 10, 2009. https://pardonmeforasking.blogspot.com/2009/11/tale-of-whale-hunt-in-gowanus-canalin.html.

15. Battle of Brooklyn

Formant, Chris. "The Maryland 400 Lost a Battle But Helped Win a War. On the 4th of July, We Should Remember Their Sacrifice." *Time*, July 4, 2019. https://time.com/5617055/battle-of-brooklyn/.

History. "British Forces Defeat Patriots in the Battle of Brooklyn." July 21, 2010. https://www.history.com/this-day-in-history/the-battle-of-brooklyn.

Old Stone House. "The Battle of Brooklyn, August 27, 1776." https://theoldstonehouse.org/history/battle-of-brooklyn/.

16. Brooklyn's Finest

Green-Wood Cemetery. "Here Lie the Secrets of the Visitors of Green-Wood Cemetery." https://www.green-wood.com/calle-installation/.

Levine, Lucie. "10 Things You Didn't Know About Green-Wood Cemetery." 6sqft. October 21, 2019. https://www.6sqft.com/10-things-you-didnt-know-about-green-wood-cemetery/.

Meier, Allison. C. "Brooklyn History: Our Famous Dead." Brooklyn Based. January 17, 2012. https://brooklynbased.com/2012/01/17/brooklyn-history-our-famous-dead/.

Murphy, Doyle. "Creepy Clown 'Haunts' Green-Wood Cemetery." *New York Daily News*, July 14, 2014. https://www.nydailynews.com/new-york/brooklyn/creepy-clown-haunts-green-wood-cemetery-brooklyn-article-1.1866552.

Wikipedia. "List of Burials at Green-Wood Cemetery." https://en.wikipedia.org/wiki/List_of_burials_at_Green-Wood_Cemetery.

17. Navy Hospital

Carlson, Jen. "Inside the Brooklyn Navy Yard Hospital." Gothamist. February 19, 2009. https://gothamist.com/arts-entertainment/inside-the-brooklyn-navy-yard-hospital.

Fabian, Ann. "One Man's Skull." Common Place. January 2008. http://commonplace.online/article/one-mans-skull/.

Find A Grave. "Naval Hospital Cemetery." https://www.findagrave.com/cemetery/2646734/naval-hospital-cemetery.

Meier, Allison. "Realm of Wounded Soldiers: Abandoned Brooklyn Naval Hospital." Atlas Obscura. May 2, 2013. https://www.atlasobscura.com/articles/abandoned-hospital-brooklyn-navy-yard.

Musings and Adventures. "10+ Haunted Brooklyn Places & Spooky Stories." September 7, 2020. https://musingsandadventures.com/2020/09/07/brooklyn-haunted-spots-spirits-spooky-stories/.

Vamonde. "Brooklyn Navy Yark Hospital." https://www.vamonde.com/posts/brooklyn-navy-yard-hospital/880.

Wikipedia. "Brooklyn Naval Hospital." https://en.wikipedia.org/wiki/Brooklyn_Naval_Hospital.

18. Wallabout Bay

Brooklyn Navy Yard. "History of the Yard." https://brooklynnavyyard. org/about/history.

Cosgrove, Benedict. "The Grisly History of Brooklyn's Revolutionary War Martyrs." *Smithsonian Magazine*, March 13, 2017. https://www. smithsonianmag.com/history/grisly-history-brooklyns-revolutionary- war-martyrs-180962508/.

Kadinsky, Sergey. "Wallabout Creek, Brooklyn." Hidden Waters Blog. June 29, 2016. https://hiddenwatersblog.wordpress.com/2016/06/29/ wallabout-creek-brooklyn/.

19. Boy Who Fell from the Sky

Dunlap, David W. "Park Slope Plane Crash: The Boy Who Fell from the Sky." *New York Times*, December 16, 2010. https://cityroom.blogs. nytimes.com/2010/12/16/the-boy-who-fell-from-the-sky/.

Park Slope Reader. "The Ghost of the Boy Who Fell from the Sky." October 14, 2012. https://www.psreader.com/the-ghost-of-the-boy-who-fell- from-the-sky/.

Singer, Noah. "Remembering the Park Slope Plane Crash of 1960." *Brooklyn Daily Eagle*, December 16, 2019. https://brooklyneagle.com/ articles/2019/12/16/remembering-the-park-slope-plane-crash-of-1960/.

Young, Michelle. "Remnants of a 1960 Park Slope Plane Crash Hidden in Plain Sight in Brooklyn." Untapped Cities. February 17, 2016. https:// untappedcities.com/2016/02/17/remnants-of-a-1960-park-slope-plane- crash-hidden-in-plain-sight-in-brooklyn/.

20. Park Slope Armory

Albrecht, Leslie. "Park Slope Armory Has Secret Tunnel and Underground Shooting Range." DNAinfo. July 29, 2015. https://www. dnainfo.com/new-york/20150729/park-slope/park-slope-armory-has- secret-tunnel-underground-shooting-range/.

Fishbein, Rebecca. "10 Facts You May Not Know About Park Slope." Gothamist. March 29, 2016. https://gothamist.com/arts- entertainment/10-facts-you-may-not-know-about-park-slope.

Miradorian. "10 Facts About Park Slope You Probably Didn't Know."
    September 12, 2017. https://www.themiradorian.blog/blog-
    posts/2017/7/10/10-facts-about-park-slope-you-probably-didnt-know.
Park Slope Parents. "The Park Slope Armory—10 Facts You May Not
    Know…." https://www.parkslopeparents.com/Hood-Pages/the-park-
    slope-armory-10-facts-you-may-not-know.html.
Wikipedia. "14th Regiment Armory." https://en.wikipedia.org/wiki/14th_
    Regiment_Armory.
Young, Michelle. "The Top 10 Secrets of the Park Slope Armory in
    Brooklyn." Untapped Cities. April 4, 2016. https://untappedcities.
    com/2016/04/04/top-10-secrets-of-the-park-slope-armory-in-
    brooklyn/3/.

21. Lincoln Plaza Hotel

Bryan, Wendy. "Heartbreak Hotel." *Village Voice*, March 24, 2004. https://
    www.villagevoice.com/2004/03/23/heartbreak-hotel/.
Jamieson, Wendell. "Memories, Draped in Red." *New York Times*, April 18,
    2004. https://www.nytimes.com/2004/04/18/nyregion/memories-
    draped-in-red.html.
Spellen, Suzanne. "Building of the Day: 153 Lincoln Place." Brownstoner.
    November 7, 2011. https://www.brownstoner.com/architecture/
    building-of-the-day-153-lincoln-place/.

22. 123 on the Park

Evans, Lauren. "Anti-Gentrification Ghosts Haunt Luxury Flatbush
    Development." Gothamist. May 19, 2015. https://gothamist.com/
    news/anti-gentrification-ghosts-haunt-luxury-flatbush-development.
Rosario, Frank, Chris Perez and Jennifer Gould. "Ghosts Scare Staff Away
    from Luxury Rental Building." *New York Post*, May 18, 2015. https://
    nypost.com/2015/05/18/ghosts-are-scaring-staff-away-from-this-luxe-
    rental-building/.
Wiedeman, Reeves. "Room with a Boo." *New Yorker*, July 13, 2015. https://
    www.newyorker.com/magazine/2015/07/20/room-with-a-boo.

23. Litchfield Villa

Casa Catherwood. "The Ghosts of Brooklyn." http://www.casa-catherwood.com/ghosts.html.

Dixon Leasing. "10 of the Best Local Haunted Houses & Spooktacular Ghost Stories." https://www.dixonleasing.com/blog/neighborhood-expert/10-of-the-best-local-haunted-houses-spooktacular-ghost-stories.

Druckman, Bella. "The Top 10 Secrets of Litchfield Villa." Untapped Cities. May 26, 2021. https://untappedcities.com/2021/05/26/secrets-of-litchfield-villa/.

24. Quaker Cemetery

Allison. "Friends Quaker Cemetery." Atlas Obscura. September 6, 2011. https://www.atlasobscura.com/places/friends-quaker-cemetery.

Beiderman, Marcia. "Neighborhood Report: Prospect Park/Park Slope; He's Here for Eternity, but Don't Ask Where." *New York Times*, September 27, 1998. https://www.nytimes.com/1998/09/27/nyregion/neighborhood-report-prospect-park-park-slope-he-s-here-for-eternity-but-don-t.html.

French, Mary. "Friends Cemetery, Prospect Park." New York City Cemetery Project. February 14, 2020. https://nycemetery.wordpress.com/2020/02/14/friends-cemetery-prospect-park/.

Geis, Shannon. "The Hidden Cemetery in Prospect Park." Bklyner. April 14, 2015. https://bklyner.com/the-hidden-cemetery-in-prospect-park-ditmas-park/.

25. Barcade

Carlson, Jen. "Boo! Barcade Was Built on Haunted Burial Ground." Gothamist. January 25, 2010. https://gothamist.com/arts-entertainment/boo-barcade-was-built-on-haunted-burial-ground.

Scouting New York. "What Happened to This Williamsburg Cemetery?" June 2, 2009. http://www.scoutingny.com/but-did-they-move-the-bodies/.

Urban Archive. "Brooklyn, 'City of Churches.'" February 2, 2017. https://www.urbanarchive.org/stories/hp4BXCNW8nY?gclid=Cj0KCQjwub-HBhCyARIsAPctr7yXHBBrabC5wefLWpb4Cfy0JVoe5Pir6udmtBLEYwvfrNqYhNStrMcaAtRBEALw_wcB.

26. The Charleston

Brooklyn Vegan. "Man Found Beaten in Williamsburg Bar the Charleston Died, Police Still Investigating." June 19, 2015. https://www.brooklynvegan.com/man-found-beate/.

Melendez, Steven. "Forgotten Spooky Sites of North Brooklyn." *Bushwick Daily*, October 22, 2013. https://bushwickdaily.com/news/1690-forgotten-spooky-sites-of-north-brooklyn/.

Yakas, Ben. "Man in Critical Condition After Incident at the Charleston in Williamsburg." Gothamist. June 14, 2015. https://gothamist.com/news/man-in-critical-condition-after-incident-at-the-charleston-in-williamsburg.

27. McCarren Park Pool

Baruch. "Reopened McCarren Park Pool Has a Haunted History." August 6, 2012. https://blogs.baruch.cuny.edu/pawprint/?p=567.

Carlson, Jen. "Body Found at McCarren Park Pool." Gothamist. July 17, 2008. https://gothamist.com/arts-entertainment/body-found-at-mccarren-park-pool.

Dixon Leasing. "10 of the Best Local Haunted Houses & Spooktacular Ghost Stories." https://www.dixonleasing.com/blog/neighborhood-expert/10-of-the-best-local-haunted-houses-spooktacular-ghost-stories.

Foderaro, Lisa W. "A Revived Pool Draws Tensions to the Surface." *New York Times*, July 4, 2012. https://www.nytimes.com/2012/07/05/nyregion/problems-at-mccarren-park-pool-have-a-neighborhood-worried.html.

Lipinksi, Jed. "The Bad Old Days at McCarren Park Pool." Politico. July 13, 2012. https://www.politico.com/states/new-york/albany/story/2012/07/the-bad-old-days-at-mccarren-park-pool-067223.

Oh, Inae. "Body Found at McCarren Park Pool." *Huffington Post*, July 28, 2002. https://www.huffpost.com/entry/mccarren-park-pool-reopen_n_1633991.

———. "McCarren Park Pool Fighting Leads to Cop Getting Punched." *Huffington Post*, June 3, 2012. https://www.huffpost.com/entry/mccarren-park-pool-fighting-violence_n_1645962.

Paranormal NYC. "1104—McCarren Park Pool Investigation." November 14, 2004. http://www.paranormal-nyc.com/1104.html.

28. Most Holy Trinity Church

Avoiding Regret. "Photo Essay: Brooklyn's Most Holy Trinity Church, Sanctuary & Triforium, Haunted." January 3, 2014. https://www.avoidingregret.com/2014/01/photo-essay-brooklyns-most-holy-trinity.html.

Haunted Places. "Most Holy Trinity Church." https://www.hauntedplaces.org/item/most-holy-trinity-church/.

Kramer, Howard. "Most Haunted Churches in the Northeast." Complete Pilgrim. October 16, 2015. https://thecompletepilgrim.com/most-haunted-churches-in-the-northeast/.

New York Haunted Houses. "Most Holy Trinity Church." https://www.newyorkhauntedhouses.com/real-haunt/most-holy-trinity-church.html.

29. St. Mazie's

Fischer. Joshua D. "Blonde Redhead Defends Their Decadence at St. Mazie." Bedford and Bowery. August 25, 2014. https://bedfordandbowery.com/2014/08/blonde-redhead-defends-their-decadence-at-st-mazie/.

Fox, Alison. "These Are the Most Haunted Places in NYC." Travel and Leisure. October 3, 2019. https://www.travelandleisure.com/trip-ideas/haunted-places-in-new-york-city.

30. Sweetwater

Greenpointers. "44 Percent Rent Increase Forces Williamsburg's Whisk to Close." April 22, 2019. https://greenpointers.com/2019/04/22/44-percent-rent-increase-forces-williamsburgs-whisk-to-close/.

Moore, Chadwick. "Flickering Lights, Strange Music and a Ghost at a Brooklyn Bar. Maybe." *New York Times*, October 27, 2014. https://www.nytimes.com/2014/10/28/nyregion/flickering-lights-strange-music-and-a-ghost-at-a-brooklyn-restaurant-maybe.html.

31. Boos and Booze

Rapley, Rob, dir. *The Poisoner's Handbook*. Arlington, VA: PBS, 2014.

32. Taphophobia

Alexa. "Being Buried Alive Was so Common in the Victorian Era that Doctors Used These 10 Methods to Prevent It." History Collection. December 23, 2017. https://historycollection.com/buried-alive-common-victorian-era-doctors-used-10-methods-prevent/4/.

Anderson Funeral Home. "The History of a Traditional Irish Wake." October 5, 2016. https://andersonfuneralservices.com/blogs/blog-entries/1/Articles/35/The-History-of-a-Traditional-Irish-Wake.html.

Bondeson, Jan. "Lifting the Lid on the Macabre History of Those Buried Alive." *Daily Mail*, March 12, 2010. https://www.dailymail.co.uk/news/article-1257330/Lifting-lid-macabre-history-buried-alive.html.

Britannica. "Body Snatching." https://www.britannica.com/topic/body-snatching.

Chi Hui Lin. "Outcry in Shanghai as Person Declared Dead and Put in Body Bag Found to Be Alive." *Guardian*, May 3, 2022. https://www.theguardian.com/world/2022/may/03/outcry-in-shanghai-as-person-declared-dead-and-put-in-body-bag-found-to-be-alive.

Jackson, Ashawnta. "History's Best Strategies for Avoiding Being Buried Alive." Atlas Obscura. October 23, 2019. https://www.atlasobscura.com/articles/users-guide-to-definitive-death.

Random Times. "What We Call Today 'Living Room,' Was Actually Called 'Death Room' in the4 Victorian Era...." January 25, 2019.

https://random-times.com/2019/01/25/what-we-call-today-living-room-was-actually-called-death-room-in-the-victorian-era/.

33. Morbid Facts

Commonplace Facts. "New Yorkers Are More Dangerous Biters than Sharks." December 18, 2021. https://commonplacefacts. com/2021/12/18/new-yorkers-are-more-dangerous-biters-than-sharks/.

Flower Patch. "6 Reasons Why Funeral Flowers Are as Important as Condolence Money." https://flowerpatchdelivery.com/blog/reasons-funeral-flowers-important/.

Fraga, Kaleena. "The Bizarre History of Sin Eaters, People Who Were Hired to Literally Consume the Misdeeds of the Dead." All That's Interesting. January 10, 2022. https://allthatsinteresting.com/sin-eater.

Halloween Series Wiki. "Michael Myers Mask." https://halloweenmovie. fandom.com/wiki/Michael_Myers%27_mask.

Irish Genealogy Toolkit. "The Origin of Halloween Lies in Celtic Ireland." https://www.irish-genealogy-toolkit.com/origin-of-Halloween.html.

Leasca, Stacey. "Why You'll Never See the 13th Floor of a Hotel." Travel and Leisure. March 9, 2022. https://ww.travelandleisure.com/hotels-resorts/hotels-no-13th-floor.

Mallinson, Harriet. "Cruise Secrets: This Bizarre Codeword Means Something Terrible Has Happened on a Ship." Express. November 7, 2019. https://www.express.co.uk/travel/cruise/1201499/cruise-ship-death-codeword-dead-body-code-word-cruises-morgue-holidays.

Mapes, Diane. "See Ghosts? There May Be a Medical Reason." NBC News. October 29, 2009. https://www.nbcnews.com/healthmain/see-ghosts-there-may-be-medical-reason-1c9926902.

Niedowski, Erika. "The Curious Creation of Left-Handed Leaders." National News. July 27, 2008. https://www.thenationalnews. com/world/the-americas/the-curious-creation-of-left-handed-leaders-1.230814.

Paranormal Investigators of Milkwaukee. "Are You Familiar with All Four Types of Hauntings?" https://paranormalmilwaukee.com/paranormal-101/four-types-hauntings/.

Robert, Embry. "What Is 'Haint Blue?' Here's Why Southern Porches Have Blue Ceilings." Today. August 28, 2017. https://www.today.com/home/what-haint-blue-here-s-why-southern-porches-have-blue-t115573.

Ronca, Debra. "What Are Witch Windows?" How Stuff Works. https://people.howstuffworks.com/witch-windows.htm.

Saxton, Jenna. "These Disney Stories Are Guaranteed to Freak You Out." All Ears. April 29, 2021. https://allears.net/2021/04/29/these-disney-stories-are-guaranteed-to-freak-you-out/.

Schwarcz, Joe. "The Real Story Behind "21 Grams." McGill. June 19, 2019. https://www.mcgill.ca/oss/article/did-you-know-general-science/story-behind-21-grams.

Taylor, April A. "Due to the Infamous 'Ghostbusters Ruling,' this New York House Is Legally Haunted." Ranker. November 24, 2019. https://www.ranker.com/list/ghostbusters-ruling-new-york/april-a-taylor.

TIME. "Louisiana: Black Is the Color…." July 15, 1946. http://content.time.com/time/subscriber/article/0,33009,803819,00.html.

Vouloumanos, Victoria. "27 Seriously Creepy Facts That, In Case You've Forgotten, Will Remind You of How Bizarre Our World Is." Buzzfeed. June 5, 2021. https://www.buzzfeed.com/victoriavouloumanos/very-creepy-facts.

Wikipedia. "God Bless You." https://en.wikipedia.org/wiki/God_bless_you.

———. "Round Barn." https://en.wikipedia.org/wiki/Round_barn.

———. "Witching Hour." https://en.wikipedia.org/wiki/Witching_hour.

ABOUT THE AUTHOR

Allison grew up in Hartford, Connecticut, and has a degree in screenplay writing from the School of Visual Arts. She is the CEO of Madame Morbid Trolley Tours, which focuses on the dark history and ghosts of Brooklyn. She also has her certificate on sommelier studies from the International Culinary Center (ICC). She enjoys history, cooking, animals, traveling and pop culture.

Visit us at
www.historypress.com